VOICES UNHEARD

VOICES UNHEARD:
Methodologically Articulated

Eds.

T. Brahmanandam

T. Bosu Babu

First Published, 2018

Published by

Kalpaz Publications
C-30, Satyawati Nagar,
Delhi – 110052
E-mail: kalpaz@hotmail.com
Ph.: 9212142040

Printed at: G. Print Process, Delhi

Cataloging in Publication Data—DK
Courtesy: D.K. Agencies (P) Ltd. <docinfo@dkagencies.com>

Voices Unheard: Methodologically Articulated / [edited by] Dr T. Brahmanandam & Dr T. Basu Babu.
pages cm
Contributed articles.
Includes bibliographical references.
ISBN 9789351282853

1. Dalits—India—Karnataka. 2. Dalits—India. 3. Dalits—Education—India—Karnataka. 4. Dalits—Education—India. 5. Caste-based discrimination—India—Karnataka. 6. Caste-based discrimination—India. 7. Women in rural development—India—Karnataka. 8. Women in rural development—India. I. T. Brahmanandam, T., T. Basu Babu, editor.

LCC DS422.C3D35 2017 | DDC 305.5688095487 23

Contents

Acknowledgment

R.D. Maurya, former Dean, School of Social Sciences and Management at B.R. Ambedkar University of Social Sciences, Ambedkar Nagar (MHOW) Madhya Pradesh has enormous experience of social exclusion. His paper "Discrimination and Social Exclusion against Scheduled Caste Students in the Institutions of Higher Learning" reveals the complex process empirically and suggests remedial measures. Going beyond this, T. Brahmanandam of Centre for Multi Disciplinary Research (CMDR), T. Bosu Babu has captured the complex emerging realities of Dalit women in his paper "Problems and Prospects of Dalit Women: An Emerging Reality." This paper provides insightful pictures with sociological imagination. Srikakolli Eliah, Subhankar Basu and Srikakolli Jayapradha Eliah Paper studies on "The Dilemma and Dialectics of the Empowerment of Women: A Sociological Deliberation". Govindaiah Godavarthi made a wonderful effort to understand the socio-linguistic of Dalit students in his study "Using Reading as a Resource to Help Dalit Students Learn English and Achieve their Desired Socio-economic Status." B. H. Nagoor of Karnataka University brings out education and health of different social groups in his scholarly study "Access to Education and Health among Social Groups: A Case Study of Migrant Slum Households of Gadag-Betageri City in Karnataka State." The paper "Violation of Dalit Human Rights-A Study in Andhra Pradesh" contributed by both Akepogu Jammanna and Pasala Sudhakar acts as a mirror to understand the issue with in-depth clarity. P.B. Desai's paper on "Status of Rural Dalit Women in India: A Case Study of Koge Village in Kolhapur District" gives an empirical pen picture well documented with facts and figures. The paper "Access to Land and Livelihoods of Rural Dalits in Dakshina Kannada, Karnataka" authored by G. Srikantha Nayaka

Ramakrishnappa. V and Vishwanatha provides us with a down to earth reality. Avinash G. Bhale brings out the political factors of exclusion in his paper "Democratic Decentralisation and nature of political exclusion of Dalits in Panchayati Raj". The much debated caste system at the backdrop of Ambedkar has been critically examined by M. Thangaraj in his paper "Ambedkar Views on Castes in India". Another paper by C. Jeroma Samraj on "Understanding the origin of inequality: People and their Access to Means Development". Kanak Kanti Bagchi has taken a retrospective view to bridge the gap between past and present in his scholarly paper "A Revisit into B. R. Ambedkar's Perception on Caste."

I am confident that this edited volume will be very helpful to all concerned. I sincerely express my gratitude to all the contributors as well as Amit Garg of Kalpaz Publications for the dedication and cordial response extended to us.

T. Brahmanandam
CMDR, Dharwad

T Bosu Babu
Advocate, Visakhapatnam

Preface

The Dalit situation in India is a cause of concern. In spite of Constitutional and Statutory provisions, Affirmative Actions, power to people through Democratic Decentralisation, etc. Dalits are in poor state of affairs. Having had concern for the same, the CMDR, Dharwad organised a national seminar on the "Dalit Situation in India: After Economic Reforms" at the backdrop of the 125th birth anniversary of B. R. Ambedkar.

The seminar was sponsored by the Indian Council of Social Science Research (ICSSR), New Delhi. The key architect of this seminar was T. Brahmanandam, associate Professor functioned as seminar convener.

It is incumbent upon all of us to retrospect the legacy of Ambedkar and the working of the Constitution as the foundation of nation state. The century old syndromes of Dalit atrocity and discrimination are still continuing in spite of special legislations like Protection of Civil Rights Act, 1955, the Scheduled Castes and Scheduled Tribes (Prevention of Atrocities) Act, 1989. The historic legacy Ambedkar fighting for social justice seems to have lost ground in neo-liberalism that has pushed the Dalits to the receiving end.

The economic reforms post-1990s and the waves of neoliberalism failed to work within the framework of a Constitutional scheme that gives right to education, right to life with dignity, right to be equally treated, right not to be exploded, etc. The Directive Principles of State Policy seems to have failed to bring the ruling dispensation out of party politics. Feminism in India doesn't address the problems of the downtrodden, and Dalit women. The so-called Left Movement got obsessed with the class struggle got lost in trade unions. The caste found a fertile ground in the resurgence of the Vedic culture. The caste-class dichotomy made the social equations more complex. The upper caste is by default the ruling class or political elite. The cultural affinities of the political elite still continue to project them as the saviour of the voiceless voters in vote bank politics. On the other hand, it has promoted a few Dalits to political elites, and they are immune from atrocities and discriminations. The Human Rights Commission supposed to be democracy's ombudsman is left with little statutory instruments. The judicial activism remains confined to Public Interest Litigation (PIL)left to the hands of individuals and organisations. The text and texture of the Dalit discourse won't match with vocabulary of the ruling elite. The much needed social reform seems to be merged into the social media from Una to United Nations. Injustice anywhere is threat to justice everywhere (Martin Luther King, Junior).Therefore, it was an academic imperative to put facts and figures into right perspectives and to come out what social sciences can contribute to this dialectics of democracy. When law falls apart and fails to protect its own subjects from being victims, what sense does it make for itself to take its own course so callously to prolong injustice by delaying justice? The 125th birth centenary of Ambedkar was a historic moment to be accountable to those left downtrodden.

There are two extremes growing unbound. On one extreme (urban), we have Indian Institute of Technologies; on the other extreme (rural), we have Industrial Training Institutes. On one extreme, we have skyscrapers; on the other we have slum dwellers. On one extreme, farmers committing suicide for not able to repay the paltry bank loans; on the other, the corporate giants enjoy lavish life style on huge bank loans. On one extreme, we have super-speciality hospitals, on the other, the primary health centres of rural India run without basic amenities. The list is pretty long. The growing disparity and discrimination have pushed the two segments to two extremes. The smart city project, growing industrialisation, shrinking agriculture, displacement of rural folk—all these suggest the validity of Spencer's axiom "survival of the fittest". Globalisation, Foreign Direct Investment, digital literacy, land acquisition, etc. will go against the rural India where majority of the Dalits live and eking out their survival. The issue is more complex than it appears.

These are the challenges before us today. The CMDR has made a humble effort to understand different facets and interfaces for a paradigm shift to realise the goals of the Constitution drafted under the Chairmanship of Dr. B.R. Ambedkar.

Keeping in view of the suggestions, the papers presented have been rephrased/edited wherever necessary. Hope this initiative to publish the papers in a book form will add value to the literature on Dalit studies and a paradigm shift.

November 2018

T. Brahmanandam,
CMDR, Dharwad.
T. Bosu Babu
Advocate, Visakhapatnam.

List of Contributors

1. **R.D. Maurya:** Former Dean, School of Social Sciences and Management, B.R. Ambedkar University of Social Sciences, Ambedkar Nagar (MHOW), M.P.
2. **T. Brahmanandam:** Associate Professor at Centre for Multi-disciplinary Development Research, Dharwad.
3. **T. Bosu Babu:** Advocate at Visakhapatnam District Bar Council Viskhapatnam.
4. **Dr Srikakolli Eliah:** Principal, Metas Adventist College, Surat
5. **Dr Subhankar Basu:** Faculty, Aljamea Tus Saifiyah, Surat
6. **Ms Srikakolli Jayapradha Eliah:** Faculty, Metas Adventist
7. **Govindaiah Godavarthi:** Asst. Professor, Department of English, Maulana Azad National Urdu University, Hyderabad.
8. **B.H. Nagoor:** Dr B.H. Nagoor, Associate Professor, Department of Economics, Karnatak University, Dharwad.
9. **P.B. Desai:** Assistant Professor, Department of Sociology, Shivaji University, Kolhapur.
10. **G. Srikantha Nayaka:** Post Doctoral Fellow, Centre for Study of Social Exclusion and Inclusive Policy (CSSEIP), Mangalore University, Mangalore.
11. **Ramakrishnappa V:** Associate Professor, Centre for Study of Social Exclusion and Inclusive Policy (CSSEIP), Mangalore University, Mangalore.
12. **Vishwanatha:** Professor at Department of Economics and Director, Centre for Study of Social Exclusion and Inclusive Policy (CSSEIP), Mangalore University, Mangalore.

13. **Avinash G. Bhale:** Asst.-cum-Asst. Director, Centre for Study of Social Exclusion and Inclusive Policy, Shivaji University, Kolhapur.
14. **Akepogu Jammanna:** Post- Doctoral Fellow at Department of History, Sri Krishnadevaraya University-Ananthapuramu.
15. **Late Pasala Sudhakar:** Former Professor, Department of History, Sri Krishnadevaraya University-Ananthapuramu.
16. **M. Thangaraj:** Former Professor and Head, Ambedkar Centre for Economic Studies, University of Madras, Chennai.
17. **C. Jerome Samraj:** Assistant Professor, Department of Economics, Pondicherry University, Puducherry.
18. **Kanak Kanti Bagchi:** Head, Department of Economics, University of North Bengal, Darjeeling,West Bengal.

1

Discrimination and Social Exclusion against Scheduled Caste Students in the Institutions of Higher Learning

— *R.D. Maurya*

"Caste is the monster that crosses ones path every way one turns"

– **Ambedkar**

"Caste is the foundation of our society; discrimination is in the air we breathe. These are our realities. "(Young Film Director Nagraj Manjule, 2016)." In the modern world education is an important vehicle of social mobility and development. The attainment of higher education facilitate the socially and economically backward community to avail the opportunities of development. Education enhances the awareness level of community about their rights, opportunities and confidence to participate in the process of development. However, for the educational empowerment of Scheduled Castes the role of welfare state and encouraging social environment is highly essential to achieve the set goals. It has been observed that the socio-cultural deprivation and caste-based discrimination and social exclusion, indifferent attitude of government functionaries and caste prejudices of teachers and fellow students create a lot of hardship, social and psychological problems for SC students in institutions of higher learning which ultimately affect their personality development, educational performance and socio-economic empowerment adversely. In higher learning institutions in general and medical, engineering and professional institutions in particular, the discrimination and social exclusion compel the Scheduled Caste students to give up their lives by committing suicide, face rustication, denial of fellowship, forced vacating of hostels and violence against them. The most burning example of social discrimination is the suicide of Rohith Vemula, a dalit student of Hyderabad Central University.

The text books are ridden with caste hegemony, the atmosphere that reinforces alienation within the campuses, classmates who take pride in their dominant caste teachers who condemn others for their miserable fates and this enact a self fulfilling prophecy of failure-these are the impossible challenges for Dalit students to surmount. Caste which ingrains the notion of intellectual superiority, when replicated within the boundaries of academia, becomes a poison potent enough to kill and consume lives.

Classrooms, instead of becoming sites of resistance and subversion, become assertions of unbridled caste power by those who believe in the twice born, sacred threads of knowledge transmission, and who are inherently obliged to maintain the status quo (Kandasamy, 2016).

Kandasamy further observed that the tiny minority of students from oppressed backgrounds who try to camouflage and masquerade out of the fear of being ostracised are punished at the time of exposure – like the mythical Karna -with the curse of fatal failure. Those Dalit students who emerge in their own right, with their identity out in the open and for all to see, become the proverbial Ekalavyas, left alive, but unable to practice their art. This is not the fate of students alone because within the corridors of caste powers, Dalit Bahujan faculty are also at the receiving end of ostracisation. As much as I have watched in awe my mother's struggle in the Indian Institute of Technology (IIT), Madras. I have also watched the absolute helplessness of the women I love crumble and disintegrate. The dismal representation of Scheduled Caste/ Scheduled Tribe/other backward classes' faculty members in our IITs/ Indian Institutes of Management(IIMs) and Universities renders the caste discrimination absolute because students from similar backgrounds do not even find a support group to hear their difficulties or give them advice.

The institutions of higher learning are not free from the shadow of caste discrimination and harassment of the students belonging to Scheduled Castes, Scheduled Tribes and other Marginalised Sections of society. The complaints were received from the students belonging to the SC\ST category in various higher education revealed the nature of caste discrimination, violence with caste abuse, intimidation/ harassment using caste abuse and award of less grades due to caste-based discrimination. In some cases even students are harassed to the extent that they take extreme steps of ending their lives by way of suicide or leave their study in between or run away from the educational institutions and ruin their bright career. The most painful and tragic incident of suicide by Rohith Vemula on January 17, 2016 in central University of Hyderabad had shaken the conscience of the people and broken the silence against the caste-based oppression, harassment and discrimination which led to nationwide protest of Dalit youths and other progressive forces of society.

The conflict in both the University of Hyderabad and the IIT Madras illustrate a deep fracture between the Hindu Right and Dalit-Bahujan ideologies, particularly those of the Ambedkarite strain, a fault line that cannot be papered over by an electoral alliance of convenience and occasional instances of power-sharing between the two sides. The Sangh Pariwar at every level, from the ruling Bhartiya Janata Party down to the Akila Bhart Vidya Parishad (ABVP), stands against equality, whether between caste, religious communities, or sexes. Instead of egalitarianism, the Hindu Right believes in an archaic arithmetic of adhikar and bahishkar, the entitlement of exclusion based on caste, religion and gender. If the Indian Republic is built on a plinth of equal citizenship, the Hindu Rashtra would be founded on ritual hierarchy and patriarchy as laid out for centuries to the caste system. Onto this unequal social order of considerable vintage would be layered a deadly neo-fascist majoritarian politics that arises out of the Hindutva imagination of the modern nation (Vajpeyi Ananya, 2016).

The incidents of discrimination, harassment and physical violence is reported against the SC/ST students in institutions of higher learning across the country. It is surprising and painful that elite institutions like IITs, IIMs, All India Institute of Medical Sciences (AIIMS), and central Universities are not free from caste Discrimination and Social Exclusion against Scheduled Caste Students... biases and discrimination against the Scheduled Caste and Scheduled Tribe students. S.K. Thorot Committee was constituted by the National Commission of Scheduled Caste, Government of India 2007, to study the problems of discrimination, harassment and suicide by SC/ST students and suggest the protective measures and congenial atmosphere in AIIMS, New Delhi. The findings of Thorat Committee are as follows:

The Committee headed by SK Thorat to inquire into allegations of differential treatment of SC/ST students at All India Institute of Medical Sciences. This was in the wake of media reports and complaints to the government about the said harassment and abuse. The committee was given the mandate to look into all matters connected with the said harassment. The AIIMS being a 100 per cent grant-in-aid government institution and suppose to comply with all the directives of the government and to provide constitutionally guarantee and safeguards to the weaker sections particularly the Schedule Castes and Schedule Tribes. The observation and findings of the committee in summary form are given below(SK Thorat Committee, 2006).

Undergraduate students

Special programmes-Absence of such programmes in AIIMS

Despite of SC/ST students insistence on remedial classes, AIIMS has not taken any initiative to arrange these classes for English language as well as basic subjects or other special courses for SC/ST students which are suppose to provide by them.

Assessment and Examination and Teachers Support to SC/ST Students

AIIMS examination system involves both internal and external assessments. A large component of the examination is highly subjective element. The examination system with 50 per cent internal assessments and with significant roles of individual faculty give scope for misuse his privilege, if he/she wishes to do so. The internal assessment and the training are linked to monitoring and hand holding process where the teacher gets the best out of the student while imparting skills and knowledge. The following responses of the students to the questions about discrimination in teaching sessions, laboratories and clinical.

Lack of consultation and interaction– About 69 per cent of the SC/ST students reported that they do not receive adequate support from their teachers and majority of the students opined the teachers inaccessibility and indifference as reason for less contact with their teachers. Nearly one-third of the students gave caste background as a reason for avoiding the SC/ST students by teachers. Thus, it emerged that the SC/ST students do not receive proper support when compared with non SC/ST students. Given the dependence of students to teachers for learning and skill, the lack of adequate support from the teachers on SC/ST students reflects in their performance and also psychological problems.

Discrimination in Teaching – Out of the total responses, 72 per cent of the respondents had said that they face discrimination in the classroom.

Evaluation of Theory Paper – About 76 per cent of students mentioned that their papers were not evaluated properly. More than 88 per cent mentioned that they get less marks than they expect in theory.

Discrimination in Practical and Viva-Voice – About 84 per cent of respondents mentioned that evaluation in practical and viva voice was unfair. About 85 per cent of them mentioned that the SC students were not given sufficient time in comparison to their counterparts belongs to higher caste students in practicals. About 40 per cent of SC students also mentioned that they get more difficult and hard questions in their practicals and viva voice. About 76 per cent of the respondents reported that the examiners do ask the caste backgrounds and this in turn affects their grades.

The self reported experiences of SC/ST students indicates that discrimination take the form of avoidance, contempt, non-cooperation, and discouragement and differential treatment by teachers towards their fellow students.

Class representatives- A representative of the class has a role in facilitating academics and even his/her role has been discriminatory.

Articulated Only on a few occasion the SC/ST students are elected as class representative. About 80 per cent of the student respondent reported differential treatment being faced in distribution of instructions like information or schedule of examination or rescheduling of classes, class trips and cultural activities.

Problem in the Hostel

Segregation in Hostel- Over a period of time and particularly in the wake of the anti-quota agitation, several students belonging to the this category of students have been shifted to top two floors of the hostel. This indirectly communicates some sort of segregation on caste lines. The SC/ST students are forced to shift to these hostels by a sustained pressure in the form of humiliation, abuse and even violence by the higher caste students. About half of the

SC/ST respondent indicated a caste harassment by higher caste students as a reason for the shifting to top floors of the hostel i.e. 4th and 5th floor.

Inter-personal relation in hostel, Mess and Dinning

1. **Social isolation-** Majority of the students living in the hostel belongs the to higher caste and maintain social isolation in their inter-personal relationship. About 88 per cent of the students reported experiences of social isolation in various ways and 84 per cent of the student respondent reported violence in various forms.
2. **Discrimination in Mess-**While the general messes are open to the reserved category students also. About 76 per cent of SC/ST respondent students mentioned that they face restrictions in joining the private messes. There is a caste division in the private mess.

Social segregation in cultural, games and sports events

Participation in games -The SC/ST students face discrimination at participatory level of various games. About 88 per cent SC/ST students face discrimination in access to basket ball as well as cricket.

Participation in the Cultural Event PULSE-The AIIMS organise a big cultural event which goes by name of PULSE. 32 per cent of the SC/ST students do not access to participated in the PLUSE event.

Nearly 68 per cent participate in PULSE on various capacities. Of these about 80 per cent participated as observer and volunteer and only 11 per cent as a competitor and 7 per cent as representatives in any committee. The SC/ST students feel that the PULSE organising committee again works on biased manner in such situations the SC/ST students do not get a fair chance to participate.

Ragging and Caste Overtone

Even though ragging is officially banned in the AIIMS, there appears to be unofficial ragging in the initial months. This has been stated by the students belongs to SC/ST category and it has serious caste overtones and several forms of humiliation are meted out to them.

Problems of SC/ST Senior and Junior Residents

There is sufficient reason and evidence including Supreme Court observations that AIIMS followed a reservation policy which is not under the guidelines of the Central Government while in selecting junior resident doctors (postgraduate students). This process effectively denies the opportunities to the SC/ST community. This should be quickly corrected. Discrimination of residents of the SC/ST category is evident in a subtle as well as direct manner. The Residents who did not cooperate with the administration in the anti-quota agitation had harrowing experiences as repercussions. The case of Ajitha Gill is a unique example.

Circumstances of the SC/ST Faculty

The roster system of selection in appointment was never followed by the AIIMS for the faculty even though it is required to follow the Central Government guidelines. This has been to the disadvantage of the SC/ST category of faculty. A recent Supreme Court order has exposed several wrong doings on the part of the AIIMS administration in the recruitment of faculty and their promotions. The SC/ST group is adversely affected by these methods of appointment. SC/ST Faculties are discriminated by the HOD's in allotting thesis guidance for postgraduate residents. This reduces their research opportunities in comparison to their non SC/ST colleagues in the publication aspect. On the other hand, Clinical opportunities are also getting reduced due to less exposure to research in this area. Conference/ workshop and external academic participation are selectively blocked in many ways for this group.

Anti-quota Agitation

The anti-quota agitation was planned by a group of people who had strong views against the reservation. Various people have given evidence to support the view that the administration of the AIIMS played a proactive role in the organisation of the agitation. The

AIIMS became the venue for the national agitation because it wants paralyse healthcare service so that it can attract public attention. Not only Paralysing of the healthcare services, they included the emergency services which would put pressure on the government to take decision on reservation. The administrative support which was widely covered in the media, to the extent of penalising and punishing those who do not support the agitation. The manner in which the Dean Deka was humiliated needs further investigation.

Discrimination in Teaching

The students were asked whether they faced discrimination in one to one teaching session in the laboratories and in practical demonstrations. Of the total responses about 72 per cent of them mentioned about some kind of discrimination being faced in the class room and only 24 per cent said no. Some students described their experience of non-co-operation by faculty in the following manner:

(a) They did not allow the SC/ST to perform the dissection.

(b) During Cadaveric dissections teachers are indifferent to them.

(c) They try to humiliate by asking a simple question.

(d) We are not given enough opportunity to perform the clinical examination or dissections.

(e) If any one is weak in the subject are not encouraged rather put down.

(f) Junior Residents are not co-operative towards. They do not explain us.
(g) Teachers are fine till they do not know the students caste. As they come to know the caste they behave differently
(h) To know it, their attitude towards you changes completely.
(i) SC/ST students are made feel to inferior in group interactions.
(j) Most students prefer to cope up in silence

Evaluation of Theory paper

The students were asked about the bias in evaluation of examination papers. Nearly 76 per cent mentioned that their papers were not examined properly. About 88 per cent mentioned that they got fewer marks than they expected. Only 20 per cent mentioned that they got feedback on their answers scripts.

Discrimination in practical and viva-voice

Only 16 per cent students were opined that the process in the practicals and viva was fair. About 84 per cent of respondent opined it negatively. The students were then asked the nature of unfairness in evaluation of practical and viva -voice.

About 85 per cent of the SC students said that they don't receive enough time with the examiners when compared to non SC students. In the same they were asked that whether the teachers make them comfortable at the time of viva-voice. More than 92 per cent of the respondent had given negative responces. About 40 per cent of the students also mentioned that more difficult question are generally put to them.

In response to the caste bias by high caste teachers, about 76 per cent of the respondent reported that the examiner had asked the caste background, about 84 per cent mentioned that their caste backgrounds are asked either directly or indirectly and about 84 per cent mentioned that their grades were affected because of their caste background.

At the level of the department, the respondents reported that the magnitude of discrimination was of higher order in Cadaveric dissections (68 per cent), followed by Microanatomy/ Histology

(60 per cent), Physiology practical (48 per cent), Biochemistry practical (40 per cent), Microbiology practical (32 per cent) and clinical examination (32 per cent) in that order. Some students described their experience of non-co-operation by faculty in following manner:

(a) The papers are marked according to the past record of the student and the impression of the students are carry forward by the teacher.

(b) The students list with their caste are supplied to the teachers.

(c) The examiners do ask the full name of the student.

(d) When SC students are failing and they humiliate him by non-SC students and Junior Residents and Senior Residents.

(e) when a similar questions are given to non SC students they score higher marks and it was observed in final year Gynecology

(f) While taking viva-voice for SC/ST students, most of the examiners make these students feel inferior and at the mercy of examiner.

(g) Some higher caste students have not even attempted full question papers, leaving about 30 to 40 per cent of question paper, they were passed with 70 per cent of marks. But SC students attempt full questions will not pass.

(h) Despite preparing hard we get less mark.

(i) The results of the last ten years in the final examination will be a testimony to the fact that reserve category students are failed intentionally and if they cleared they pass marginally.

(j) Even if they do well, they will never score more than higher caste students of same acumen.

The National Scheduled Caste Commission has appointed a Single Member committee under the Chairmanship of B.L.Mungekar (former member of the Planning Commission) to look into the allegations of caste discrimination faced by scheduled caste students at the Vardhman Medical College, Delhi. The committee has brought certain hard fact in this college on discrimination. The committee has examined the every aspect of the case and ensure that the guilty would be brought to book.

Mungekar discovered to his dismay that not only 35 scheduled caste students failed repeatedly in one particular subject i.e., physiology – but the authorities never bothered to meet the students and address their grievances. He had to resort to RTI to seek information and approach the high court to ensure their rights as equal students. As his report puts it, the faculty of the said department 'resorted to caste-based discrimination and neglected the duties assigned to them, not by omission but by commission'. Even the other administrative staff, including the head of the institution, had shown interest to intervene and settle the problem. Not only did the students lose years because of this apathy, shockingly, the same authorities were guilty of showing leniency towards general category students. While they had no qualms about barring scheduled caste students from taking their examinations due to lack of attendance, four students from the general category, who were detained for inadequate attendance, were allowed to take the examination.

Mungekar, who has finally submitted his report, has put forward wide-ranging recommendations. Apart from asking the authorities to pay compensation of '10 lakh to students like Manish and others who had moved to court — underlining the fact that 'the mental trauma that they had undergo is not measurable in terms of money'— he has demanded that legal action under the Scheduled Caste and Scheduled Tribe (Prevention of Atrocities) Act, 1989 be taken against former Principal V K Sharma and his then colleagues Shoma Das, head of the physiology department, Principal Jayshree Bhattacharjeė and Raj Kapoor, professor of physiology, and a liaison officer.

It is worth highlighting that this was not the first time the college had made the national headlines. Two years ago, the Delhi High Court intervened on a writ petition filed by aggrieved students of the college. Twenty-five scheduled caste students who had taken admission in 2004 and 2005 approached the court when it was discovered that they were deliberately being failed in physiology. Under instructions from the High Court the college was forced to conduct fresh examinations; 24 students out of the 25 passed.

Last year too, a committee of experts belonging to the All-India Institute of Medical Sciences (AIIMS) and Lok Nayak Jaiprakash

Narayan Hospital (LNJP), headed by L R Murmu, looked into ongoing discrimination at the college had found that in the last five years all the students who had failed the physiology paper belonged to the backward/scheduled castes. Murmu noted in his report how a student had failed three years consecutively only with one mark. Other members of the committee also noted how all the students who had failed the physiology paper had performed well in other subjects and had got admission in the college because of their high marks.

There are many similar cases in other reputed institutions in the capital.

Take the premier medical institute in the country, AIIMS, which is always in the news headlines for their wrong doings. In 2010 and 2011 two students committed suicide — Balmukund Bharti and Anil Meena. Both belong to the scheduled caste category, and their suicides again raised the issue of treatment to the scheduled caste students in this institution. The institute had made headlines earlier too, when caste discrimination cases forced the National Commission on Scheduled Castes to appoint a committee to investigate the complaints. The committee acknowledged that scheduled caste students do face discrimination in AIIMS and it had suggested some recommendations on the treatment of SC students. It has been a long time since the report was handed over to the government, but there have been no concrete moves to end the discrimination. Some months ago it was disclosed that the said report had been scrapped!

A story in the national daily Mail Today ('Caste Aside: AIIMS Junks Report Nailing Discrimination at Institute', May 15, 2012) revealed how the 'institute has decided to junk a report…which had recommended action against several officials including a former director…The commission in its report submitted in 2008 had specifically named the then director P Venugopal for indulging in caste discrimination and for being the 'main actor' in the anti-quota stir which had plagued the institute for several days'. Despite the commission's strong recommendation that action against the then director be initiated under the Scheduled Caste and Scheduled Tribe (Prevention of Atrocities) Act, AIIMS preferred to junk the report citing the strange logic that, "the institute had come over the phase of unrest and a congenial atmosphere was prevailing".

All these votaries of a 'congenial atmosphere' would not like to be reminded about the herding together of reserved category students, which a leading daily reported about: 'Parts of AIIMS hostels are turning into SC/ST ghettos. Reserved category students said they were being "hunted out of the remaining rooms" by upper-caste students and driven to two floors of the hostels,' (The Telegraph, July 5, 2006). Graffiti in one of the rooms of an SC student in the hostel warned the occupant to 'get out of this (hostel) wing'. The SC/ST students also shared with the reporter how they are 'failed' in the examinations if they dare complain against the discrimination. The sub-dean of the institute, himself a scheduled caste member, corroborated what the students were saying.

Denial of action against guilty teachers and the consequent lack of closure for aggrieved students at a premier institute like AIIMS reminds one of the refusal of the administration at Chikitsa Vishvavidyalay, Lucknow (Lokmat, April 2, 2012), to implement an order of the SC commission in matters related to the deliberate failing of dalit students in a particular subject. In fact, the aggrieved students and V K Gupta, vice-chancellor of the said university, were jointly summoned by the commission to sort out the matter on March 13, 2012, where the VC had agreed in principle to allow the Dalit students to write their examinations in the next session. It's a different matter that he refused to abide by the instructions of the commission and started threatening the dalit students. One of the students, Neeraj, subsequently attempted suicide but was saved in time. It is strange that these students were failing a particular subject only, at this university.

Merely three years ago, the Supreme Court had to intervene in a case related to scheduled category students from IIT-Delhi and instruct the administration that it could not expel students merely on the basis of performance. Responding to a petition filed by Avinash Bagdi and five other scheduled category students, the court said students who had got into IITs after going through a long admission process, could not be externed, violating the principles of natural justice. A Supreme Court bench of K G Balakrishnan and P Sathasivam asked the

IIT administration to arrange special classes for the students so that they could catch up with general category students. The said petition had specifically mentioned how callousness on the part of the administration had made the whole system of reservations meaningless as neither were such students provided with the necessary facilities nor were they given special coaching which resulted in over 90 per cent of scheduled category students either failing their first or second years and leaving the institute, or being expelled because of 'below par performance'.

A close look at the academic atmosphere at other IITs makes it clear that IIT-Delhi has been no exception. A story in Tehelka (June 16, 2007), that focused on IIT-Chennai, explained how the institute had metamorphosed into a 'modern-day agraharam' (in Tamil, a brahmin's house is called an agraharam). The author gave figures explaining how the quota of seats meant for reserved category students always remained underutilised. The figures were 11.9 per cent for SC students (2005) when it should have been 15 per cent. At the higher education level, the ratio is further reduced: in research one finds merely 2.3 per cent, and for PhDs, 5.8 per cent.

This discrimination is not confined to the student level; the authorities or higher-ups, with their Varna mindset, also see to it that eligible candidates from socially oppressed sections are not allowed to become teachers. Take IIT-Kharagpur (Times of India, September 12, 2012, 'Quotas Fail to Break Caste Ceiling in IITs'), one of the oldest IITs; it has only three scheduled caste professors, two associate professors and two assistant professors. There is not a single scheduled tribe person at all the three levels. There are two OBC (other backward classes) professors and seven assistant professors but no associate professor. Coming to the general category, there are 227 professors, 105 associate professors and 165 assistant professors.

Despite the fact that Tamil Nadu has a background of social movement, under-representation of marginal castes and scheduled tribe members prevails. While there are 212 professors, 91 associate professors and 177 assistant professors in the general category, the figures are 3, 3 and 44 for the SC category. A lone ST is assistant professor; there are seven assistant professors from the OBC category.

Consider AIIMS, there is ongoing legal wrangling related to the recruitment of 164 associate professors in the institute. The petitioners' contention is that the authorities clearly violated all n while appointing these teachers. Despite the matter being subjudice, and despite an affidavit filed by the central government and the institute administration in court which clearly acknowledges that there had been violations of rules in the appointments, the administration had no qualms about promoting some of them.

It was only last year that Ghulam Nabi Azad, health minister of the UPA government, informed Parliament that around 500 posts in the reserved category at Safdarjung Hospital, Ram Manohar Lohia Hospital and Lady Hardinge Hospital, Delhi, were lying vacant because of the absence of 'suitable candidates'. There was no uproar over the fact that all these hospitals that face a tremendous rush of patients are short of 500 doctors.

The plea of 'absence of suitable candidates' while making selections under the reserved category is regularly invoked when there is a lapse on the part of the higher-ups in sticking to their constitutional responsibilities. In fact, the reason lies elsewhere. If we consider hospitals or medical colleges, on the one hand it is the logical culmination of an absence of sensitivity and lack of consciousness among the higher-ups as far as the rights of oppressed students are concerned, or the resistance put up by a section of them opposed to affirmative action of any kind; and on the other hand it is a product of the economic policies being followed under a neo-liberal regime. As usually observed, the free play of market forces results in cutting necessary subsidies or contractualisation/casualisation of labour; thus doctors too are appointed for a limited period.

The disinclination of appointing teachers from these categories is not only limited to the medical field. There have been reports from different news papers suggests that(Times of India, September 6, 2012) SC/ST teaching positions are lying vacant in all the central universities. In fact, in all the central universities more than 32 percent teaching posts were of sanctioned to SC/ST however, only 4.18 percent potions are occupied these groups. The list includes premier institutions like Delhi University (DU), Jawaharlal Nehru University, Aligarh Muslim

University (AMU), Benaras Hindu University (BHU) and University of Hyderabad. Here, vacancies exist in all three categories — assistant professor, associate professor and professor (Gatade Subhash, 2012).

The study conducted by the author on the impact of the Scheme of "Post-Metric Scholarship to the Scheduled Castes in Gujarat 2007 reveals that the Scheduled Castes students are the victims of caste based discrimination and harassment in different ways in educational institutions of higher learning in Gujarat.

Table 1: Whether experienced Caste based injustice or discrimination in the Educational institutions

S. No.	*Respondents response*	*Number*	*Per cent*
1.	Yes	50	25.00
2.	No	150	75.00
	Total	**200**	**100.00**

It was found that there were 25.0 per cent Scheduled Caste students experienced the caste-based discrimination in educational institutions. They were of the opinion that the practice of caste-based discrimination and injustice still practice against the Scheduled Castes in society. Gujarat is developed state economically yet it is not free from caste prejudices and discrimination against SCs.

Table 2: Types of discrimination and harassment faced by SC students in higher education institutions

S. No	*Types of discrimination and Harassment*	*Numbers*	*Percentage*
1.	Insult us by saying inferior caste	2	4.00
2.	Improper treatment given by the educational institutions	2	4.00
3.	Some officers deny to attest the forms to be submitted for Post-Matric Scholarship	2	4.00
4.	Undignified behaviours and social discrimination affects on performance of University results and SC students score less marks in examinations	3	6.00
5.	People utters caste-based comments that hurt our sentiments	2	4.00

(Contd...)

6.	Even today we are considered untouchable and the practice of untouchability is being practiced against us	2	4.00
7.	Caste discrimination all over	3	6.00
8.	We could not get respect in educational institutions	2	4.00
9.	Because of we being scheduled caste we are given less marks in term examinations and proper guidance and teaching is also not provided them	2	4.00
10.	The high caste students never asks us about our problems and also the teachers never pay proper attention towards our	2	4.00
11.	Difficulties in study	1	2.00
12.	The majority of offices belonging to other castes carries mental carries biasness against the SCs and they consider us low	3	6.00
13.	During primary education the primary teachers kept us away from them	1	2.00
14.	The primary teachers did not pay proper attentions to the Scheduled Caste students	4	8.00
15.	The students have been harassed and the Office staff also do not respond properly towards their problems	1	2.00
16.	In villages the SC students gets water to drink from distance	2	4.00
17.	If they know that we belongs to SC then our admission are being made very late and also the scholarship is provided very late	3	6.00
18.	The other caste students keep distance from the Scheduled Caste students, and they do not make friends with them	3	6.00
19.	The teachers force us to sit on the last row in the class room	1	2.00
20.	When our friends come to know that we belong to SC then they start avoiding our friendship	2	4.00
21.	They do not allow us to enter into temple and their houses	1	2.00
22.	Even if there is no direct injustice but we experience it indirectly	1	2.00
23.	The students are never informed about the scholarship even it is received by the Colleges	2	4.00
	Total	**50**	**100**

As the above table-2 reveals that they do practice of social discrimination and injustice in the educational institutions of Gujarat.

The injustice and discrimination experienced by SC students in many ways and most of them experienced the practice of untouchability. There were students respondents who were of the opinion and reported that SC students were not treated with dignity and honour and they are still consider as inferior and get insulted on the basis caste. The government functionaries, teachers and fellow students do not cooperate with Scheduled Castes students and insult by uttering caste-based comments. The respondents also reported that every stage of life they have to struggle for survival, the social and economic problems always haunt them and they have to study under tension in adverse conditions. For getting Post-Matric scholarship, poor SC students have to run from post to pillar for fulfillment of formalities. The student respondents were of the opinions that anti-Scheduled Caste environment in the academic institutions adversely affects their performance and level of achievement in higher education.

Table 3: Whether there is caste discrimination experienced in hostels by the SC students

S. No	*Respondents response*	*Numbers*	*Percentage*
1.	Yes	50	25.00
2.	No	150	75.00
	Total	**200**	**100.00**

Table 4: Types of discriminations practiced against the Scheduled Caste students in hostels

Sl. No.	*Types of discrimination*	*From Whom*	*Number*	*Per cent*
1.	The high caste students tease us saying that we get admission only because of reservation, it hurts our feeling. They also say that your percentage is very low	Upper caste students	5	10.00
2.	Considering us untouchables we are not allowed to go further and discriminated at every step		2	4.00
3.	The discrimination is open. Sometimes the high caste people do it openly in a large groups		3	6.00
4.	They discriminate in hostels, as well as other places at high level indirectly		6	12.00

(Contd...)

5.	The high caste students stay in separate rooms they do not stay along with the Scheduled Caste students		3	6.00
6.	They do not behave properly with us due to our poor conditions		2	4.00
7.	We are harassed by the high caste students in hostels		2	4.00
8.	Even today we are not allowed to touch their utensils and water etc in hostels		3	6.00
9.	Upper caste students practice untouchability against SC students at the time of eating together		11	22.00
10.	The high caste people look at us with biased mind		4	8.00
11.	All those who stay in a hostel belongs to Scheduled Caste, they come from different state, hence some time we had arguments, tension within us also		4	8.00
	Total		**50**	**100.00**

As reflected in the above table, different types of ill-treatment and harassments perpetuated by the upper caste students, teachers and officials against the SC students in academic institutions and hostels of Gujarat. There were 22 per cent SC students reported that untouchability is practiced against them overtly and covertly in the hostels. It was revealed by the some SC students that in hostels high caste students do not share rooms and stay along with Scheduled Castes students in the hostel rooms. The respondents also reported that whenever identity is disclosed by the SC students people start negatively and they change their attitude towards SC students. Some of the respondents told that even today SC students could not touch the utensils and water and other eatables of upper caste students.

Conclusion

To get rid of caste discrimination, there is a need for the annihilation of caste and to establish egalitarian social order as envisaged by Ambedkar during his struggle for the emancipation of downtrodden sections of Indian society. The unity of Dalit, Adiwasi, bahujan and other progressive forces of Indian society is the need of hour to defeat the discriminatory and sectarian forces who divide people on caste, religion and gender to maintain the status quo in the society. It is also necessary to implement the UGC formulated a new set of Regulations that empower into revoke, recognition, or even withdraw grants to public and private colleges and Universities if they failed to prevent the harassment and victimisation of SC/ST students at the hands of their teachers and peers as defined. The regulations, called UGC (Prevention of Caste-Based Discrimination/Harassment Victimisation and Promotion of Equality in Higher Educational Institutions) Regulations 2012 — which were approved by the Human Resources Ministry, Government of India.

References

Sukhadeo Thorat, K.M. Shyamprasad, R.K. Srivastava (2006), Report of the Committee to enquire into the Allegation of differential treatment of SC/ ST Students in aims.

Kandasamy Meena, (2016), He has left us with only his Words, The Hindu, January 19, 2016, New Delhi, p. 11.

Yamunan Sruthisagar, (2016), Grim Shadow of Caste over Educational Institutions in T.N., The Hindu, January 22, 2016, New Delhi, p. 12.

Subhash Gatade, (2012), Dronacharyas All: Caste Discrimination In Higher ducation, 16 October, 2012 Retrieved from http://www.countercurrents.org/gatade161012.htm

Vajpeyi, Ananya, (2016), Ancient Prejudice, Modern Inequality, The Hindu, January 20, 2016, New Delhi, p. 10.

Joshi, Namrata, (2016), New Voices but not enough Voices, The Hindu, January 23, 2016, New Delhi, p. 11.

Raghunath, Sujatha, (2016), Delaying Scholarship for Dalits is also Discrimination, The Hindu, January 24, 2016, New Delhi, p. 9.

Maurya, R.D., (2007), An Evaluatory study of Post-Metric Scholarship and its impact on Scheduled Castes Education in Gujarat, (Unpublished), BRAUSS, Ambedkar Nagar (MHOW), M.P.

2

Problems and Prospects of Dalit Women: An Emerging Reality

— T. Brahmanandam & T. Bosu Babu

Traditionally, India is known for the caste-based social system having its foundation rooted in Hinduism. The hierarchal-based social order has its legacy in the Manusmriti. While addressing the nature of the caste system, J.H. Hunton observes that it is exclusively an Indian phenomenon and no other society in the world can be compared to the caste-ridden society of India (*http://shodhganga.inflibnet.ac.in/bitstream/10603/8562/8/08_chapter%203.pdf*, p.1). This social structure is not just based on purity and pollution; it has also accorded other aspects of human life which is coupled with landlessness, poverty and degrading occupations. Therefore, it is a discriminatory and exploitative structure.

The hierarchal system has implicated certain groups being untouchables by birth and they have been discriminated and ill-treated even today. Under this traditional scheme of caste system, the untouchables who happen to be at the bottom of the society face social apathy, vulnerability and discrimination in spite of constitutional and statutory provisions of equality, reservations, and special safeguards. The people identified with untouchability were never treated as human beings and denied basic human dignity. They simply exist as slaves for the higher castes or means for their welfare and luxury. They still suffer from a stigma of untouchability which to a great extent constitutes their social identity though they are struggling for an equitable selfidentity.

In a caste-ridden society like ours, the untouchable families mostly in rural areas lead their life without any assets, and they are mostly landless agriculture labourers or small artisans. It has been noticed that 82.8 per cent of the land of our country is owned by the upper caste Hindus. It is estimated that only 7 per cent of the land is owned by the Dalits, and among them, nearly 70 per cent have less than one hectare. Studies even suggest that the competition in India is not based on talents and natural aptitudes but on the basis of castes in which one is born. In such a situation, the majority of the lower strata are unemployed or underemployed; they get the very meagre wages from their employers. Due to these prevailing conditions, they fall into a debt trap and resulted in them into bondage. Dalits are denied basic necessities like drinking water and public places by the powerful upper castes which are the worst form of dehumanisation. They are left with no voice and choice. They are the victims of violence and atrocities both at home and outside (*http://shodhganga.inflibnet.ac.in/bitstream/10603/8562/8/08_chapter%203.pdf, p.11; Accessed on 27/10/16*).

To reduce the gap and promote socio-economic advantages in the society, the Government of India has passed a number of legislations in favour of these groups under Affirmative Action Policies (AAP). Along with these, it has also created certain constitutional safeguards under Article 17 that deals with the abolition of untouchability, Article 341 notifies the Scheduled Caste and ensure their fundamental rights, and the Directive Principles of State Policy authorises the state to protect these socially marginalised group from any further discrimination in the society based on their caste. In addition to these, the Government of India has enacted certain special laws to remove discriminatory practices against the Scheduled Castes and also to ensure their social and economic empowerment. The anti-discriminatory measures like the Untouchability Offence Act of 1955 (renamed as the Protection of Civil Rights Act [PCR] in 1976), and the Scheduled Castes and Scheduled Tribes Prevention of Atrocities Act (POA) of 1989 were enacted to prevent crimes and atrocities against Dalits. Permanent national commissions have been set up to safeguard their rights for both SCs and STs as well as for women (*Sabharwal, Nidhi, Sadana and Sonalkar, Wandana.* p. 46). Despite all these laws, the vulnerabilities have been reported on regular basis. In India, across castes women considered to be inferior to men and being Dalit women she has to face much more vulnerabilities than their men folk. The problems of Dalit women are different from Dalit men. Dalit women, she faces triple discrimination than their men folk. As a Dalit, she faces untouchability, being a woman she faces gender discrimination and as a woman she cannot work equally with men and earn lesser wages which are inner side of the discrimination (*Mahey,* p. 149). On the other side, Dalit women are not only discriminated by the people of higher caste but also within their own community. Within community men dominate her. (*Ruth Manorama,* p. 1). By simply applying, these aforesaid laws will not render any relief to the Dalit women. Based on the above understanding, the proposed paper on 'Development of Dalit women in India: Problems and Prospectus' would try to study the following:

1. What are the socio-economic factors that have influenced the marginalisation of Dalit women?
2. To what extent has the feminist movement played a positive role towards Dalit women?
3. Have the Dalit women utilised educational opportunities of government sufficiently to improve their socioeconomic conditions?

The paper is based on the secondary data which consists of books, articles, National Sample Survey Organisation (NSSO) reports, government reports including census data. The paper has three sections, the first section is on historical background, the second section is on the feminist movement and their role in the upliftment of the Dalit women, and the last section will be of government programmes and their impacts on Dalit women.

B.R. Ambedkar, popularly known to be the chief architect of Indian Constitution and social reformer of modern India made a pioneering contribution to reform the Hindu social order. In his 'Annihilation of Caste' (1932), he questioned the Hindu social order. He fought relentlessly throughout his life to reform the Hindu social order and particularly to improve the conditions of the underprivileged and women in Indian society. He wrote extensively to counter the views of gender relations sanctioned by the *Shastras* and upheld by Hindu traditions. In his writings like "*The rise and fall of Hindu Women*", "*The Women and Counter-Revolution*", "*The Riddle of Women*" and "*Castes in India: Their Mechanism, Genesis and Development*" have analysed the manner in which gender relations are artificially constructed under the Hindu social order which not only moulds the upper caste mindset towards their women but also conditioned women to behave in a submissive way that would be suitable for domestic and family responsibilities (*Bijay,* 2014, p. 393). At this backdrop of suppression, struggle, and torture, what the Dalit women face in their everyday life are much more severe. All these hardships are not merely based on their economic or educational status, it was directly imposed on them by the upper caste (Hindu) patriarchy and that has been legitimised by the Hindu religious scriptures.

Brief Review of Literature

Bharati's (2014) paper is on the exploitation of Dalit women and their portrayal by Telugu Dalit poetess in their poetry. The paper suggests that the Dalit women get exploited in the name of caste and sex. It further says that both Dalit women and Afro-American girls are viewed as sex objects without any compunction on the part of the males of the dominant culture. The author argues that the oppressive system took a long time to accept Dalit men's ability and creativity in literature, and it would be much more difficult for Dalit poetess. The author has compared the non-Dalit feminists with US feminists. However, in the case of Black feminism and Dalit women feminism, the antiimperialism, anti-caste and anti-racist ideologies are the prime targets. It suggests that until 1980, the writings of majority Telugu Dalit women had the Aryan and Christian perspectives. The atrocities on Dalits in Andhra Pradesh has changed the Telugu Dalit women writings in response these incidents. To portray the Dalit women condition, the author has used all the available Telugu Dalit women poetry. While concluding the paper, the author concluded with an observation that the Dalit (male) intellectuals and leaders along with non-Dalit men and women look at Dalit women only as women, an object of exploitation but never miss a chance to exploit Dalit women in every possible way. Hence Dalit women poets have to fights for the rights of Dalit women through their poetry.

Dinesha's (2014) paper is on the political reservation at the local level. The 73rd Constitutional Amendment has created space for Dalit women in PRIs. This Act has also empowered them to redress their grievances. However, in reality, they are not fully involved in decisionmaking process due to a number of problems such as caste-based discrimination on Dalit women representatives. There is bureaucratic indifference towards these elected representatives. The same Act did not ensure them to function effectively. The study also noticed that owing to the lack of education, they fail to take independent decisions on many issues. Another important point is that wherever Dalit women function effectively in such places, they get most vulgar and abusive language and sometimes allegations also from their opponents.

Ashalatha (2013) explains the position of Dalit women in Indian society. They are the largest segregated group in the world. Dalit woman, consider to be Dalit among Dalits and suffer three-fold oppressions on account of gender, caste i.e., 'untouchable', and finally class as they hail from the poorest among the marginalised communities. The paper argues that the so-called Hindu religious books are solely responsible for their visible miseries. It also submits that the process of globalisation has brought many severities to their life like mechanisation of harvesting and transplantation that has forced the Dalit women of their traditional work in the agricultural sector. The abject poverty has pushed them into the sex trade to earn their livelihood. Hence, government intervention is necessary to help and protect their girls for overall development and reduce the poverty among these groups.

Roy Burman (2012) state's that the status of tribal women is better in comparison to women in general society. The sacerdotal/ artificial Hindu social order that characterises the Hindu culture is absent among the tribal groups. Though the tribes to have preference of son, they don't go for sex determination tests; nor do they practice female foeticide or infanticide. To reveal the status of the tribal women in society, Roy-Burman gave examples of Kasis, Moppilas, Todas of

Nilgiri, Jaunsaris. He has elaborately discussed different marriage practices and the position of women. Since tribal women are considered to be an asset, there is the practice of bride price at marriages which is quite common among them and in sharp contrast to the practice of general caste-Hindu. He made some observations on tribal women and their economic activities such as fishing, weaving, and selling fruits and forest products in the weekly markets. The tribal area of *Betul in Madhya Pradesh*, the collection, and marketing of firewood is the domain of tribal women. There have been significant changes among the tribal women in the North-Eastern region mostly led by the Protestant Church.

Badri Narayan (2004) deals with the cultural repression of Dalits and their place in Hindu society. He has narrated the rise of the Dalit leadership in North India, especially in Uttar Pradesh. The author says the Dalits also replicated the upper caste formula of glorification the past memories and images which have brought a sense of pride among Dalits and the political consciousness. The glorification has forced them to construct a positive identity and self-respect in a world of ravaged with power, conflict and competition. In the method of glorification, he has referred three women heroes (Viranganas) of the 1857 rebellion, namely, Jhalkaribai, Udadevi and Mahaviridevi and their images and contributions were used effectively to build Mayawati image. The same method has popularised the Mayawati's charismatic image on one side and encouraged the growth of leadership among Dalits on the other. To build grass-roots level political consciousness among dalits, they used two methods, one is popular tales…and another one is the plightof Dalits. He also argues that the statues…that have been installed in public places, specifically in places where the Dalit population is more has generated deeper impacts on Dalits. Lastly, he says that the way *Bhartiya Janta Party* has used the gods, heroes and other cultural resources to mobilise their electoral support in a similar way the *Bahujan Samaj Party* has also used their past glories in a similar way. He is of the view that Dalit memories and images gave an alternative reading in which it may be regarded as replication rather than Sanskritisation.

Ammu Josep's (2004) paper is a review of 'Dalit Women in India: Issues and Perspectives'. The reviewer makes a modest attempt and suggests that the existing movements- be it feminist movement or Dalit movement have failed to address Dalit women problems. In such circumstances, this volume is a great contribution to highlight their problems and generate some consciousness on their issues. An attempt was also made in the volume to explain the term Dalit. It says that Dalit women have both qualities to generate leadership as well as consciousness to the feminist movement. Since they have the quality to generate leadership, visualised an autonomous and independent platform to enable and address their special needs and forge their own identity as Dalits and as women. In such a situation, the National Federation of Dalit Women (NFDW) was launched in August 1995. The founders made it clear that it doesn't want to fight separately rather it calls for a strong alliance between the Dalit movement and women's movement. This evolved an understanding and linkage between three sets of players. The paper also suggests that the early phase of women's movement was dominated by the upper castewomen from urban centres and therefore their actions and perceptions were very limited. Because of their privileged position, they failed to recognise the patriarchy as an ideology of social system that institutionalise gender-based differentiation and discrimination. It was Dalit women assertiveness that made other women in the movement change their voices and concern and set their priorities. There is no doubt that Dalit women were primarily responsible for bringing out this positive development within the women's movement. Due to this, the Fifth National Conference has given highest priority to Dalit and Tribal women issues. This implies that they are clearly moving beyond the presentation and analysis of their cause in Dalit Women in India and arguing their own case both realistically and forcefully.

Mahipal (2004) says the 73rd Constitutional Amendment Act has facilitated an adequate space to Dalits including Dalit women to get elected to these bodies. However, while discharging their duties, they face a number of problems. To identify and address these problems, a workshop was conducted at Haryana Institute of Rural Development (HIRD) in collaboration with National Commission for Women (NCW). Nearly 118 elected representatives have attended the workshop. At the workshop, almost all the Dalit women representatives have raised their concerns and the problems posed by male members of the panchayats and village people belonging to higher castes. On the whole, illiteracy and lack of awareness have constrained them to function. It also concludes that most of the representatives are not aware of various schemes specifically meant for the welfare, education and economic development of Dalits. Wherever the Dalit women representatives are literate, they are more assertive than the others. On the whole, it can be treated as the beginning to end of indivisibility of Dalit women sarpanches in local governance.

Vimal Thorat (2001) opines that the Dalit women's issues are consciously ignored both by the Dalit movement as well as women's movement. Many times Dalit movement/politics gets identified with caste politics, and it deliberately resists the gender dimension of the caste. This indicates the patriarchal attitude of sidelining or ignoring women from the decision-making bodies. Her study highlights the problems faced by Dalit women in her day-to-day life and it further says that Dalit women not only suffer from gender inequalities but inequalities within inequalities. Though Dalit women have been part of larger feminist movement, but they repeatedly experienced the apathy of the elite feminist movement to address the issues of Dalit women. Nevertheless, the Dalit women's assertive articulations are growing. The formation of the National Federation of Dalit Women in 1995 has created space for their voices and issues. The study has also presented the case studies of elected Dalit women representatives *(sarpanches)* from Haryana and Rajasthan.

Gopal Guru's (2000) paper is on marginalisation. His paper has raised three questions? Why the process of marginalisation is taking place among Dalits? How and why does it continue to exist among Dalits? Lastly, is it culture specific? Among all, the political marginalisation is the most important because no political party is with Dalits and their issues during the elections. He further says if Dalits get elected to political hierarchy, they would only get plum portfolios. This practice continues to exist from the days of Ambedkar. The cultural marginalisation enforces the Dalit students and teachers at educational institutions to behave in a ghettoised manner. Due to this, they didn't get access to the larger teaching community. He has raised a very important subject like public employment opportunities. In public employment, Dalit men and Dalit women generally can't aspire beyond to menial jobs like sweepers, scavengers, and coolies. Similarly, in the field of politics, the Dalit leaders try to replicate the same cultural hierarchy against their own Dalit women whose participation in the political process has never been acknowledged and never liked by the Dalit patriarchy.

Swaroopa Rani (1998) argues that literacy gave chance to the untouchables to attack the centuries-old oppression. The Dalit selfrespect has destroyed the *Sanatana* traditions. Those denied basic human rights have stormed into literary avenues and ruling the Telugu literature. They try to make some clarification on who are Dalits and what is Dalit poetry? Whose poetry is Dalit poetry? It submits that those who represent oppression and are critical to Dalit poetry. Before Joshua, there were a number of revolutionary poets, and it was only Joshua who was considered as the first Dalit poet and his 'Gabbilam' (the Bat) the first poem. He was the trendsetter in Telugu Dalit poetry for condemning the caste system. It was Ambedkar's anti-caste movements and incidents, such as Karamchedu, Chunduru, and Padirikuppam that led them to write poetry against this oppression. She further says that their poetry not only remains confined to literary activities, but also exposes the day-to-day humiliations faced by Dalits.

The poetry written by Dalit women can only bring greater impact than the poetry written by Dalit men or upper caste women. There are references to thirteenth century poet Molla and his *Ramayana*. The paper also highlights on the contemporary Dalit feminist writers. There are narrations from Challapalli Swaroopa Rani's *'Mankenapuve' and 'Vegu Chukka,* Darisi Sasi Nirmala's '*Dalituralu* and *muttugudda Kapputunn*'*;* and Vijayalakshmi's *'Pani Pila'*. All these poetic narrations are dealing with how Dalit women are treated outside her home. There are poems that have explained uncivilised practices like *Jogini, Devasi, Basvi*. The same poetry also narrated a Dalit Nurse in the hospital, a Dalit woman agriculture labour. Finally, the paper concludes that all these poetic writings should move from poetry to short stories and novels to bring a change in the system and society.

With this brief literature, the paper tries to study the socio-religious practices and its impacts on Dalit women and also assesses the role of feminism in developing Dalit women, and lastly, how the educational policies and political decisions have impacted their development.

Socio-religious practices

The Hindu Sastras and Puranas have denied educational and property / wealth rights to women. However, in the case of Dalit women, it not only denied these rights but denied Dalit women as human beings rather than treated them as sex objects and promoted child marriages. The same *Sastras* and *Puranas* consider the killing of a dalit woman as a minor offence. (*Ashalatha.* 2013, p. 1).

The socio-religious practices have serious implications on Dalit women. Under this custom, temple prostitution continues to exploit Dalit women. It is one of the controversial practices in Telangana, Maharashtra, and parts of northern Karnataka. Though this practice is banned by law, every year the young Dalit girls dedicate/ secretly to get married to the goddess and marked as devadasis. These girls are then sexually exploited by the upper-caste landlord and rich men of the village. Most of the devadasis in Karnataka belong to the untouchable Madiga community. A recent study shows that almost 94 per cent of the girls who dedicate to village goddess are less than 15 years. Once they are devoted to village goddess, they are more like commodities over which others can transact. Despite the Devadasi Prohibition Act in all these states, the number keeps on increasing. In 1993-94, their number was 22,873 in Karnataka. In 2011, their number has gone upto 23,787. This shows that all the rehabilitation schemes have failed to curb the devadasi practice in the state (*Pinto,* 2014, pp. 68-73).

Purity and pollution

Dalit women have been relegated to a life of inequality from the moment she born on the earth. Due to certain specific jobs, occupations and type of works continue to be assigned to them on the basis of their hierarchical status (*Sharma,* 2015). Despite a law on prohibiting the use of manual labour to dispose human excreta, the manual scavengers are still existing in many parts of India. As per 2011 census, more than eight lakh people are engaged in clearing night soil by hand and they earn less than ‘ 2000 per month. Remunerations of these workers are meagre and work guaranteed is nil (*Acharya,* p. 2). These kinds of works have relegated Dalit women to more and more deprivation, social exclusion and discrimination.

The same purity and pollution has excluded Dalit women, and they are hardly employed as cooks at upper caste homes. The pilot study of Benerjee and Sabharwal (2013) has brought out a few hard facts in this regard. In a sample of 216 women with respect to access to the labour market of Delhi, the study suggests that only 37.40 per cent of Dalit women are engaged as cooks, while in the case of general women, it is more than 62.6 per cent. This suggests that Dalit women face difficulties in getting employment in cooking and other household jobs because of the notion of purity and pollution (*Sabrwal,* 2015, p. 254). The same pilot study concludes that Dalit women are mostly employed as domestic helpers like sweeping, mopping and dusting works. For details see the table below.

Table 1: Discrimination in hiring for type of work

Type of Work	*Dalit Women*	*Upper-Caste Women*	*Total (N=216)*
Cooking	37.40	62.6	100
Washing utensils	41.0	59.0	100
Washing clothes	57.3	42.7	100
Cleaning (dusting, sweeping, and mopping)	62.5	37.5	100

Source: Banerjee and Sabharwal, 2013; data computed from fieldwork, March to May, 2013.

The same purity and pollution concept has barred the Dalit women from being employed as mid-day meal cooks in government schools. The news has been reported by *The India Express* (*Bengaluru edition*) on November 6, 2015 that the upper caste people have stopped sending their children to a government school in Kolar just because a Dalit woman was appointed to cook mid-day meal. A similar story has also been reported where the present Chief Minister Shri Siddaramaiah studied. Due to the sustained efforts supported by official interventions, children of all castes eat mid-day meal prepared by Dalit women (*The India Express, 6th Nov. 2015, Bengaluru Edition*).

Feminism and Dalit Women

The brutal patriarchy and their oppression, gender discrimination and sexual violence are the key factors responsible for the feminist movement in India. It is also true that these forms and methods have forced the women to be treated as unequal citizens across the world and more particularly in India. In these circumstances, feminism developed in the 1970s as a new forum/platform to raise the voice unheard and share their experiences that all women sufferings are essentially the same and they want to establish equal economic, social and political rights for women (*Sowjanya,* p. 1). Due to this, the mainstream movements of Indian women continue to be led by the privileged/dominant caste including the educated women. This may be the possible factor for the non-representation or marginal representation of the voices of Dalit women in the so-called feminist movement. According to Sharmila Rega quoted by Singh (2014), "there was thus a masculinisation of and a savarnisation of womanhood, leading to a classical exclusion of Dalit womanhood" (*Singh* 2014, p. 40).

According to Prasad quoted by Tomar (2013), "we have been denied the right to articulate our own visions of emancipation. Our energies have been co-opted to working out the visions of dominant others who have shown scant respect of our world–view or philosophy of life, by not enabling us to articulate them or work towards achieving them". (*Tomar,* 2013, p. 2). It further suggests that Dalit women are perceived as 'others' because of the centuries old Brahmanical values. On the other, the globalisation has brought more and more privileged and professionally educated young people whose services have been hired for women's issues (*Stephen Cynthia in Counter Currents.org.* 16 Nov. 2009). As the ground situation is against Dalit women, many activists and scholars including Ruth Manorama argue that the modern feminist movement has recognised patriarchy as the sole responsible factor for all kinds of sufferings of women, and it only addressed domestic violence and dowry deaths which are confined to the urban middle-class, and it never addressed the caste-based atrocities, rape, and sexual assault by the upper caste men. Stephen argues that the Indian feminists consider violence caused by only patriarchy, and they have not given much importance to the caste-based violence. In such a situation, a new wave of feminism developed in 1990s with individual identity as a focal point. They rejected the universalisation of experiences of women belonging to different castes and classes. This

49 led to the emphasis on independent identity of Dalit women and this has also enhanced their articulation levels (*Thorat, 2001*). According to Gopal Guru quoted by Singh in his article, 'Dalit women talks differently' suggests that to understand Dalit women, one needs to delineate both the internal and the external factors that are linked their life and livelihood. The internal factors are Dalit patriarchy or control, and the external factors are castes, caste-based atrocities, rape and unequal wages (Singh 2014, p. 40).

According to Shweta Singh, the struggles of Dalit women are similar to that of the Black Americans. In both the situation, their interests were represented by non-discriminators and had only token appearance in the movements. Like Dalit women, black women were doubly oppressed because they were women, and they were black. Though they had played an equal role in the movement for liberation from slavery, they never got a similar status as men even after slavery was abolished. A similar fate can be noticed in the case of Dalit women like their black women counter-parts America. They had little influence while struggling for their rights and rightful position in the society (*Ibid,* p. 41).

The idea of feminism in India was started to achieve sisterhood, but in their approach and activity, the presence of Dalit women is almost negligible. Due to this, the Dalit women representatives might have thought of having their own organisational set up to address their problems in the society (*Sharma,* p. 7, *http://ijellh.com/violenceagainst-dalit-womena-human-right-concern, Accessed on 18/11/16*). The anti-Mandal agitation was also an important factor for the birth of Dalit feminism in India. During the anti-Mandal agitation, most of the feminists were against the implementation of the Mandal Commission recommendations in favour of the OBC. The logic to oppose the reservations to the OBC was that there had already been 22 per cent reservation to the SCs and STs. The additional 27 per cent reservation to the OBC would, in all likelihood, deny the upper castes of their due opportunities to get jobs. Hence, they opposed all kinds of reservation to save the nation from the hands of the unmeritorious groups. In this context, the upper-caste women represented themselves as 'non-submissive', 'assertive' as they say that they have the social responsibility to save the nation in the pretext of merit. This assertion of the upper-caste women had the latent connotations of caste and patriarchy behind their manifest lamentation on the death of merit due to reservations. This implies that they supported the caste-based social system which strictly forbade the caste exogamy, and secondly, it also implies that they were economically and socially dependent on their husbands, i.e., upper-caste men. Moreover, the arguments that Dalits are less meritorious also reflect their caste prejudice. This protest brought the question of caste question within the category of women. (*Sowjanya, p.3, http://tiss.academia.edu/SowjanyaTamalapakula,* Accessed on 18/11/16).

Dalit feminism opposes Marxism as it never recognises the caste and gender; rather it recognises only class. While in India, caste and patriarchy are the licences for all kinds of atrocities against women and more particular against Dalit women. Dalit feminism is the outcome of Dalit women's experiences. Atrocities committed on Dalit women in the name of religious customs, culture, and social norms are the main concerns of Dalit feminists (*Narayankar* 2014, p. 8).

Educational Impact on Dalit Women

The responsibility of the government has increased after independence particularly in promoting the educational interests of the Dalits and other marginalised sections. In the beginning, the government attempted to increase the number of primary schools. However, the same trend could not continued in 60s and 70s due to increasing importance on quality education. Between 1983 and 2000, improvements in access to education for all have been made, although the difference between Dalit women and general women remained constant. In this period, the enrolment rate of Dalit boys has increased from 47.7 per cent to 63.25 per cent whereas upper castes males enrolments has jumped from an already relatively impressive 73.22 per cent to 82.92 per cent. The same progress has not been observed in the case of Dalit women from 15.72 per cent to 32.61 per cent, when compared to their upper-caste counterparts whose enrolment climbed from 43.56 per cent to 59.15 per cent. Although large scale improvements have been noticed in enrolment rates in India, statistics show that very little progress has been made in decreasing the education gap between castes (The Dalits of India: education and Development, Erik Fraser. http://www.e-ir.info/2010/06/23/the-dalitsof-india-education-and-development/). Besides low literacy rate, the problem of high drop-out rate has been registered among Dalit girls. The percentage of drop-outs at the primary, middle, and secondary levels in 2009-10 was quite high compared with the upper- caste girls. Because of the high drop-out rate at the primary and middle stages, enrolment at the higher stages of school and college level is extremely low from these sections.

Conclusion

Since independence, the process of democratisation has increased the responsibility of the government manifold. Education is the potent (independent) variable to the development of human resources. The Ministry of Education at the Centre has been renamed as the Ministry of Human Resource. Keeping this in mind, the Right to Education has been given the status of Fundamental rights, and necessary provisions have been made for the children (up to 14 yrs.) to have free education, if parents fail to provide so. Education or human resource is understood in a binary framework; if people are not resourceful, they are liabilities. In the absence of the social security system in place, it's imperative to be resourceful and self-reliant. The demand for education has grown mostly because of technological advancement in economy that has forced us to live in software society. In this race for the survival of the fittest, Dalits, of course, are lagging behind necessary resources, but they are aware of what makes Dalits discriminated and exploited. The efforts of cultural industry will provide Dalits with "feel-good" fictions, but the critical school will keep on questioning the growing gaps, better say disparity, between the principles embodied in the Preamble and the practice of the same Constitution when it comes to Dalits. The Dalit unrest (including Dalit feminism) has questioned the very legacy of law and order. The so-called (elite) feminism is growing on Facebook and in literary festivals. On the contrary, the Dalit feminism is gaining ground not only in reaction to caste and/or patriarchy, but also in sociological imagination linking individuals to larger history of social structure.

References

Acharya, S. Sanghmitra. (2016). 'Dalits in Conservancy and Sanitation Works: Exploring the connects between Economic Reforms and Their Health' paper presented in a National Seminar on Dalit Situation in India: After Economic Reforms at Dharwad from April 21-22.

Ammu Josep (2004). Touch Me, Touch Me Not: Gender, Caste, and the Indian Women's Movement (*Review Article*). *Contemporary Sociology,* Vol. 33, (6). pp. 654-657.

Ashalatha. (2013). (*Paripex – Indian Journal of Research,* Vol. 2 (2). pp. 254-256.

Bharati, T. (2014). *Telugu Dalit Women Poets: The Distinctive Voice against Caste and Gender Discrimination*, in *Counter Cultural Discourse and Dalit Literature in India.* Edited by M. Dasam and Rajesh Karankal, ABD Publishers, Jaipur.

Bijay K. Barnwal. (2014). B.R. Ambedkar's Quest for Gender Equality: it's Relevance in Contemporary Feminist Discourse. *Online International Interdisciplinary Research Journa*l. (Bi-Monthly). Vol.IV (II). pp. 393-399.

Borooah, Vani Kant, Sabharwal. Nidhi Sadan, Diwakar, G Dilip, Mishra, Vinod Kumar, and Naik, Ajay Kumar. (2015). *Caste, Discrimination, and Exclusion in Modern India*. Sage Publications, New Delhi.

Burman, Roy. (2012). Status of Tribal Women in India. *Mainstream.* Vol. (12) March 10. *https://www.mainstreamweekly.net/article3314.html. Accessed on 22/11/2016*.

Bandhu, Pranjali. "Dalit Women's cry for liberation: My Rights are Rising like the Sun, will you deny this sunrise? Edited in Anupama Rao." Caste and Gender, Kali for Women", New Delhi. 2003. pp. 109-110.

Dinesha. (2014). Dalit women Panchayat Representatives and Social Exclusion: Myth or Reality? *KILA Journal of Local Governance.* Vol.1 (1). pp. 15-22.

Fraser, Erik. The Dalits of India: education and Development. *http://www.e-ir.info/2010/06/23/the-dalits-of-india-education-and-development/Accessed on 22/11/2016.*

Guru, Gopal. (2000). Dalits from margin to margin. *India International Centre Quarterly*, Vol. 27(2). pp. 111-116.

Manorama, Ruth. Background information on Dalit women in India, *http://www.rightlivelihoodaward.org/fileadmin/Files/PDF/Literature_Recipients/Manorama/Background_Manorama.pdf. Accessed on 23/6/2016.*

Mahey, Sonia. The Status of Dalit Women in India's Caste Based System. *University of Alberta, http://www.dalits.nl/pdf/StatusDalitWomen.pdf. Accessed on 23/5/2016.*

Narayan, Badri.(2006). *Women heroes and Dalit assertion in North India (Cultural subordination and the dalit challenge):* Sage Publications, New Delhi.

Narayankar, Tej. (2014). Anger and Protest as the Symbol of Dalit Feminine Concept. *Research Front.* Vol. 2(1). pp. 7-12.

Pal, Mahi. (2004). Caste and Patriarchy in Panchayats. *Economic and Political Weekly*, Vol. 39*(32)*. pp. 3581-3583.

Pinto. (2014). Dalits in Karnataka: In Search of Identity and Equality. Manak Publishers. New Delhi.

Rani, Swaroopa. Challapalli. (1998). Dalit Women's Writing in Telugu. *Economic and Political Weekly,* Vol. 33(17). pp. WS21-WS24.

Sabharwal, Nidhi Sadana and Wandana Sonalkar. Dalit Women in India: At the Crossroads of Gender, Caste, and Class. *Global Justice*: *Theory Practice Rhetoric* (8) 2015, pp. 44-73.

Singh, Shweta. (2014). Representation of Dalit women in Dalit men's and women's autobiographies. The Delhi University *Journal of the Humanities and The Social Sciences.* Vol. 1. pp. 39-46.

Sharma, J.K. Violence against Dalit women: A Human Right Concern, p. 7, http://ijellh.com/violence-against-dalit-womena-human-right-concern, Accessed on 18/11/16.

Status of Dalit Women: A Review

http://shodhganga.inflibnet.ac.in/bitstream/10603/8562/8/08_chapter%203.pdf.Accessed on 27/10/16.

Stephen, Cynthia. (2009). Feminism and Dalit Women in India. Counter Currents.org, http://www.countercurrents.org/stephen161109.htm. Accessed on 27/8/2016.

Sowjanya, T. Understanding Dalit Feminism. p. 3. http://tiss.academia.edu/SowjanyaTamalapakula, Accessed on 18/11/16).

Tomat, Ruch.(2013). Dalit Feminism: A Transformation of Rejection into Resistance. The Criterion An International Journal in English. Vol. 12. pp. 1-8

Thorat, Vimal. (2001). 'Dalit women have been left behind by the Dalit movement and the women's movement'. *Combat Communalism,*

https://sabrangindia.in/article/%E2%80%98dalit-women-have-been-left-behind-dalit-movement-and-women%E2%80%99s-movement%E2%80%99. Accessed on 23/11/2016.

This is how a Karnataka village stopped discriminating against a Dalit cook in a govt. school. Indian Express, 6th Nov.2015, Accessed on 20/11/2016.

3

The Dilemma and Dialectics of the Empowerment of Women: A Sociological Deliberation

— Dr Srikakolli Eliah, Dr Subhankar Basu, and Ms Srikakolli Jayapradha Eliah

Introduction

Let's begin with an analogy from literature.

There was an old woman
Who lived in a shoe.
She had so many children;
She didn't know what to do.

There is a new version, though anonymous, reflecting the empowerment of women.

There was a young woman
Who lived in a shoe.
She had no children;
She knew what to do.

A few questions are to be addressed to understand women empowerment. Why women empowerment? Is it just a feminist slogan?

Can Marxism be extended to gender exploitation? Is it a movement challenging patriarchy? In the existing power structure, isn't the family a safe place for women? Is it the demand of the (patriarchy) family to liberate women in order to have less liability? Is it for the extra economic benefit of the family the housewife is to work outside in the name of empowerment? Is it good or bad for the family system? Can it be the realisation of gender equality as a result of democracy over six and a half decade? Is it the result of the discourse on feminism on social media? Is it the resurgence of the feminist cult of goddess Durga and Kali in mythology or Cleopatra and Catherine in ancient history or Indira Gandhi, Medha Patkar, Kiran Bedi, Sobha De, etc. of modern India? The list can be pretty long. It may be otherwise a mere creation of imitation as fashion. Can women empowerment be understood as anomie? Can it be the product of the interfaces of state and society resulting in structuration? Is it the gender conflict restructuring the family system? How is that (extra) power to be exercised? What role would women have? Where is social empowerment possible in the existing social structure, organisational framework, and social action? What is the model of empowerment? How is empowerment taking place? How is it reciprocated? There can be other questions too. These are just random questions that one is expected to look into. However, the most important question is the space where this empowerment possible. It has to be in the social space—be it institutional framework with reference to status and roles or the formal organisation where a lower caste Dalit woman can be the boss of a Brahmin man working as an accountant in the same office? It is also possible for a Brahmin boy to fall in love of a Dalit girl and have romance on the sea beach or dine together in a posh hotel. Empowerment of women cannot take place in an empty space. Romance and love making can very well be captured with phenomenology. But more amazing than anything is the plight of women amidst empowerment.

Now, let's try to understand the dilemma and dialectics of the empowerment of women in India from sociological perspectives. Durkheim (1952) suggests that man is almost entirely the product of society, while woman is to a far greater extent the product of nature. Expanding on these observations, he says of man: his tastes, aspirations and humour have in large part a collective origin, while his companions are more directly influenced by her organ-ism. His needs, therefore, are quite different from hers. In other words, women and men have different identities, tastes and inclinations because women are less socialised and are closer to nature than men. Giddens (2006:110) is not ready to accept such a claim, stating that the female identity is as much shaped by socialisation as that of males. If women's social position and identity are mainly shaped by their involvement in reproduction and child-rearing, then differences of gender are deeply embedded in all societies. Why is this discrepancy in power between men and women in different societies? Here is the study: female genital mutilation in Iraqi-Kurdistan an empirical study by wadi to understand the discrepancy of the rights of women in African countries (http 1).

To give it a theoretical perspective, let us recall what Marx (1875) wrote as the critique of the Gotha Programme:

> Rights can never be higher than the economic structures of society and its cultural development conditioned thereby.

Putting this remark to Engel's *Family, Private Property and State* and the so-called Marxian perspective on family, it becomes ample clear of the position of women in the African countries being at the receiving end. The question is how far India is different when the traditional authority is still holding the social system? Though state is run by the rational legal authority, the society is still under the traditional authority. Marriage, divorce, and inheritance take place under the provisions of personnel laws framed by the respective religious communities. The Uniform Civil Code is still a distant dream even in digital India.

Opposite to the functional stands the conflict paradigm. The classical conflict is mostly structural. Between the polar opposites (functional and conflict) stands the action theory with subjectivity and creativity of social actors to construct society. Many women feel empowered of Kiran Bedi or Sunita Williams and accordingly construct their interactive patterns. While putting the threads of structure and action together, Giddens (1984) comes out with the theory of structuration that is taking place in women empowerment. It's a complex structuration in which actors get divided and stands opposite on the basis of gender; the traditional authority (society) stands opposite to rational legal authority (state). Moreover, phenomenology and feminism have distinct overviews on the empowerment of women in interactive spectrum. Feminism has led to an assault on the sociological theory and methodology. Not only has the male domination of sociology been challenged, but there have also been demands for a comprehensive reconstruction of the discipline itself—both the questions that form its core and the presentation of discussions surrounding them (Giddens 2006:111). The structure and content of discourse also affect the women empowerment. In the Nirma detergent advertisement, while pushing out the car stuck in mud slit, Hema, Jaya, Sushma, and Rekha proved themselves superior to menfolk standing there. Why should only boys have fun, is the popular slogan in the advertisement of pleasure bike.

From the gender perspective, all women belong to a single category. However, other categories like class, caste, religion, economy, education make them stand divided. The upper caste Brahmin women and the Dalit women do not enjoy the same social status in society. The women belonging to the two extreme echelons of society do not confront with the dilemma and dialectics of the empowerment of women. It‘s the literate and liberal middle class women who confront with the dilemma and dialectics of empowerment.

Women empowerment cannot be understood without reference to social structure, social action, culture, and power to assess to the dilemma and dialectics of empowerment. There are a few key institutions constitute the core of society. Law is one of them. There are ample laws giving the women the scope of empowerment. There are questions as to why it comes from the state and not from the society. Are women endangered? The slogan *Beti Bachao and Beti Padhao"* needs government patronage. The depleting sex ratio of women is another question of concern.

The principle of gender equality is enshrined in the Preamble, Fundamental Rights, Fundamental Duties, and Directive Principles of State Policy. The Constitution not only grants equality to women, but also empowers the State to adopt measures of positive discrimination in favour of women. India has also ratified various conventions and human rights instruments committed to equal rights of women. Key among them is the ratification of the **Convention on the Elimination of All Form of Discrimination against Women (CEDAW).** The CEDAW was the first document to comprehensively address women's rights within political, cultural, economic, social and family spheres. The 1993 **Declaration on the Elimination of Violence against Women (DEVAW)** set forth ways in which governments should act to prevent violence, and to protect and defend women's rights. Let's consider the constitutional and statutory provisions of the empowerment of women. The following articles of the Constitution are meant to be for the protection and promotion of women:

Constitutional Provisions

- Equality before law for women (Article 14)
- The State not to discriminate against any citizen on grounds only of religion, race, caste, sex, place of birth or any of them (Article 15 (i))
- The State to make any special provision in favour of women and children (Article 15 (3))
- Equality of opportunity for all citizens in matters relating to employment or appointment to any office under the State (Article 16)
- The State to direct its policy towards securing for men and women equally the right to an adequate means of livelihood (Article 39(a)); and equal pay for equal work for both men and women (Article 39(d))
- To promote justice, on a basis of equal opportunity and to provide free legal aid by suitable legislation or scheme or in any other way to ensure that opportunities for securing justice are not denied to any citizen by reason of economic or other disabilities (Article 39 A)
- The State to make provision for securing just and humane conditions of work and for maternity relief (Article 42)
- The State to promote with special care the educational and economic interests of the weaker sections of the people and to protect them from social injustice and all forms of exploitation (Article 46)

- The State to raise the level of nutrition and the standard of living of its people (Article 47)
- To promote harmony and the spirit of common brotherhood amongst all the people of India and to renounce practices derogatory to the dignity of women (Article 51(A) (e))
- Not less than one-third (including the number of seats reserved for women belonging to the Scheduled Castes and the Scheduled Tribes) of the total number of seats to be filled by direct election in every *Panchayat* to be reserved for women and such seats to be allotted by rotation to different constituencies in a *Panchayat* (Article 243 D(3))
- Not less than one- third of the total number of offices of Chairpersons in the *Panchayats* at each level to be reserved for women (Article 243 D (4))
- Not less than one-third (including the number of seats reserved for women belonging to the Scheduled Castes and the Scheduled Tribes) of the total number of seats to be filled by direct election in every Municipality to be reserved for women and such seats to be allotted by rotation to different constituencies in a Municipality (Article 243 T (3))
- Reservation of offices of Chairpersons in Municipalities for the Scheduled Castes, the Scheduled Tribes and women in such manner as the legislature of a State may by law provide (Article 243 T (4))

Legal Provisions

- The Crimes Identified Under the Indian Penal Code (IPC)
- Rape (Sec. 376 IPC)
- Kidnapping & Abduction for different purposes (Sec. 363-373)
- Homicide for Dowry, Dowry Deaths or their attempts (Sec. 302/304-B IPC)
- Torture, both mental and physical (Sec. 498-A IPC)
- Molestation (Sec. 354 IPC)
- Sexual Harassment (Sec. 509 IPC)
- Importation of girls (up to 21 years of age)

Crimes identified under the Special Laws (SL)

- The Employees State Insurance Act, 1948
- The Plantation Labour Act, 1951
- The Family Courts Act, 1954
- The Special Marriage Act, 1954
- The Hindu Marriage Act, 1955
- The Hindu Succession Act, 1956 with amendment in 2005
- Immoral Traffic (Prevention) Act, 1956
- The Maternity Benefit Act, 1961 (Amended in 1995)
- Dowry Prohibition Act, 1961
- The Medical Termination of Pregnancy Act, 1971
- The Contract Labour (Regulation and Abolition) Act, 1976
- The Equal Remuneration Act, 1976
- The Prohibition of Child Marriage Act, 2006
- The Criminal Law (Amendment) Act, 1983
- The Factories (Amendment) Act, 1986
- Indecent Representation of Women (Prohibition) Act, 1986
- Commission of Sati (Prevention) Act, 1987
- The Protection of Women from Domestic Violence Act, 2005

Special Initiatives for Women

- **National Commission for Women:** In January 1992, the Government set-up this statutory body with a specific mandate to study and monitor all matters relating to the constitutional and legal safeguards provided for women, review the existing legislation to suggest amendments wherever necessary, etc.
- **Reservation for Women in Local Self-Government:** The 73rd Constitutional Amendment Acts passed in 1992 by Parliament ensure one-third of the total seats for women in all elected offices in local bodies whether in rural areas or urban areas.
- **The National Plan of Action for the Girl Child (1991-2000):** The plan of Action is to ensure survival, protection

and development of the girl child with the ultimate objective of building up a better future for the girl child.

- **National Policy for the Empowerment of Women, 2001:** The Department of Women & Child Development in the Ministry of Human Resource Development has prepared a National Policy for the Empowerment of Women in the year 2001. The goal of this policy is to bring about the advancement, development and empowerment of women.
- **The National Credit Fund for women known as Rashtriya Mahila Kosh (RMK)** was set up by the Government of India in 1993 as a national level organisation under the Ministry of Women and Child Development to meet the credit needs of the poor and asset less women in the informal sector.

Welfare Schemes for Women

- Rajiv Gandhi Scheme for Empowerment of Adolescent Girls
- Indira Gandhi Matritva Sahyog Yojana
- Support to training and employment programme for women
- Hostel for working women
- Women empowerment and livelihood programme in Mid-Gangetic Pains
- Swadhar (Scheme for women in difficult circumstances)
- Scheme for combating trafficking
- Family counselling centre
- Short stay home programme
- Awareness generation programme
- Condensed course of education for adult women
- Integrated scheme for women's empowerment
- Gender budgeting scheme

Here is the real dilemma. Why are there so many laws to protect and empower women? Law in sociology is an institution. Law can be defined as codified values. The values are broad based and vague. The values require norms, little more specific, for practice. However, when values do not work in a given society, laws are invoked as they are the authoritative allocation of values. The values related to gender equality do not work in Indian society. Therefore, values are codified and hence authoritatively allocated. The next question is about making and implementation of laws. Everyone should be consulted equally in determining policy by which they are affected. Women empowerment, if at all, has to have the women's participation in making their own laws. This question takes us directly to the debates and deliberations of the Women's Reservation Bill in Parliament. What is more surprising is that in spite of so many laws, women at large are not at par with their male counterpart in a state run with rule of law. Barker (1951:101) comes out with a critical observation: Authority gives validity to law, and justice gives it value. Laws may be devoid of justice, but jurisprudence itself is in (credibility) crisis. When law falls apart and fails to protect its own subjects from being victims, what sense does it make for itself to take its own course? The textures of social conflicts and criminal jurisprudence do not match. Law may have its own jurisprudence, but *khap panchayats* prefer to go for instant retribution. What emerges is the subservience of the institution called state to society which is intrinsically and inherently patriarchal. This discussion is left with a question whether family is safe for women. Domestic violence and divorce rate can be the credible indicators that will be discussed further. In addition, educational and nutritional disparities also pose sufficient data to understand empowerment.

The violence against women may be linked to the knowledge system and practices through which we build and recognize gender identities (Goffman 1977). Bourdieu (1998) has developed an analytical perspective to describe how differences are built, acted on and reproduced. The socially legitimate patterns of identity and behaviour are social constructions. The organisation of society is built upon and sustained by social practices and gender roles. Amnesty International argues that violence against women is a violation of human rights that cannot be justified by any political, religious, or cultural claim. A global culture of discrimination against women allows violence to occur daily and with impunity (http 2).

Some Grim Realities of Women Empowerment

- 11 women die after sterilisation surgeries in Chhattisgarh (The Hindu November 11, 2014) If someone has died of sterilisation, something grave has gone wrong, Kate Gilmore, the Deputy Executive Director, United Nations Population

- Sex ratio falls to 898 girls per 1,000 boys. Despite the 2011 census setting alarm bells ringing about India's worsening sex ratio, the gap between male and female registered births in India fell further in 2012 and 2013, new official data suggest (The Hindu, Oct. 17, 2015).
- In its 2012 report on Gender Equality and Development, the World Bank estimated that over the last two decades, around 2.5 lakh girls were killed in India each year because of their sex (World Bank Report 2012) (The Hindu, March 25, 2014).
- When marriage is less than sacred. The Union Minister of State for Home Affairs Haribhai Parathibhai Chaudhary said marriage in India is a sacrosanct institution. The concept of marital rape is not suitable in the Indian context due to illiteracy, poverty, social customs, values, religious beliefs, and other factors (The Hindu Centre for Politics and Public Policy: June 15, 2015).
- Mulayam's shocker: Boys will be boys, they make mistakes… Will you hang them for rape? (The Indian Express, April 11, 2014).
- India's sex industry includes some 2 million sex workers, 20 per cent of which are under age 16 and considered children, though different laws use different age limits (Sen 2004). The nature of trafficking differs across the 28 states within India. Trafficked persons are exploited in a wide variety of ways. These include use of victims for bonded labour, domestic work, agricultural labour, begging, organ trade, adoption, forced prostitution, entertainment, forced marriages, and child soldiers? (Human Trafficking in India: Dynamics, Current Efforts and Intervention Opportunities for the Asia Foundation (http 3).
- Many women have no say in marriage (The Hindu, March 18, 2014)
- According to figures released by the National Crime Records Bureau (NCRB), the total number of rape cases reported in

India has gone up to 33,707 in 2013 from 24,923 in 2012. In 15,556 cases, the rape victims were aged between 18 and 30 years in 2013.

- 77 per cent of girls in India face sexual violence by partner (The Hindu, September 6, 2014)
- The NCRB data for 2013 shows that 1.3 lakh people committed suicide that year. Among suicides by women, a whopping 51.4 per cent are committed by housewives (almost 23,000), despite the fact that the non-worker and marginal worker female population engaged in household duties make up only 33 per cent of the entire female population, according to the 2011 Census (The Hindu June 15, 2015).
- The Global Gender Gap Report by the World Economic Forum in 2014 has ranked India 114th out of 142 countries that scores 0.646 (0.00=inequality, 1.00=equality). In 2006, the gender gap was 98 (out of 115 countries) and the score was 0.601
- In its 2012 report on Gender Equality and Development, the World Bank estimated that over the last two decades, around 2.5 lakh girls were killed in India each year because of their sex(The Hindu, March 25, 2014)
- There is a gender divide, with women and girls enjoying less access to information technology than men and boys. This can be true of rich and poor countries alike. United Nations Secretary-General, Kofi Annan Statement to the World Summit on the Information Society, Geneva, 10 December 2003
- Sex ratio falls to 898 girls per 1,000 boys (The Hindu, October 17, 2015).

Some Glossy Pictures of Women Empowerment

- Lloyd Unisex Washing Machine.
- African Union declares 2015 the Year of Women's Empowerment
- 28 Year Old Woman Driver Steers Chennai's First Metro Train (HuffPost India June 29, 2015).

- Companies with women board members make more money (The Times of India, Oct. 27, 2014).
- Women top online buyers of personal stuff (The Times of India, Dec 31, 2014).
- Women now demand their right to orgasm (The Times of India, August 24, 2014).
- SC allows unwed mother to apply for child's guardianship. In a progressive judgment, the Supreme Court on Monday allowed an unwed Hindu mother to apply for guardianship of her minor child without taking consent from the child's father (The Hindu July 6, 2015).
- Most Powerful Businesswomen in India 2014 (Business Today).
- Women angel investors in Chennai: Sangeetha Kandavel profiles six women angel investors who are active through the Chennai Angels network, in the belief that backing a venture with timely resources and mentorship can make a huge difference (The Hindu, March 14, 2015).
- Empowerment of Women through Self Help Group. With 74 lakh SHGs covering over 10 crore households with saving balance of over Rs. 7, 000 crore as on 31 March 2011. (NABARD Circular).
- Muslim women opposed to unilateral divorce (The Indian Express, August 9, 2015).
- Women Prime Minister, women Chief Ministers, ministers, MPs, MLAs, Governors, women judges, diplomats, professionals, CEOs, etc.
- Over a thousand women professionals from different walks of life came together at the Swami Vivekananda 150 Women Convention 'on 23rd January 2014 in Chennai to discuss on Indian woman as the guide for the world at crossroads'. On its panel, there was a host of leading women personalities (The New Indian Express, Jan. 25, 2014).
- 72% city women prefer nuclear families (The Times of India, November 5, 2009).

- Maharashtra nods for women on night shifts. As of now, no woman can work in any factory except between the hours of 6 am and 7 pm. After the Act is amended, women can work from 7 pm to 6 am. (The Times of India, May 21, 2015).
- Women's universities and colleges in India: Almost every state in India has a women university and colleges.
- The BBBP is an acronym but not very popular. It stands for *Beti Bachao, Beti Padhao*, a popular political slogan. This slogan is due to an alarming call of depletion child sex ratio (CSR) between 0 to 6 years of age. It has shown decline from 976 in 1961 to 918 in 2011. It reflects pre-birth discrimination manifested through gender biased sex selection and post-birth discrimination against girls. The societal norms of dowry, lineage, last rites, property and inheritance for son have led to gender based discrimination and violence (http 4).

Dilemma and Dialectics in Empowerment

- Maharashtra tops in number of women arrested for murder (The Times of India, Sept. 21, 2015)
- Make prostitution legal: Women's panel member (Times of India: July 10, 2015).
- Abortions by U-15 Mumbai girls up 67 per cent. Abortions among teenage girls below the age of 15 in Mumbai have recorded an alarming 67% spike in 2014-5. Civic data accessed through an RTI further shows that out of nearly 31,000 women who opted for medical termination of pregnancy, 1,600 were below the age of 19 (The Times of India, May 14, 2015).
- India's 100 richest includes only four women. Only four women feature in this year's Forbes list of 100 richest Indians (The Hindu, September 24, 2015).
- Women's Rising Employment and the Future of the Family in Industrial Societies. Becker's (1981) theories of marriage and family behaviour hypothesize that women's increasing labour force participation has had a critical and presumably irreversible impact on the family. Parsons (1949), who argued

that sex-role segregation is a functional necessity for marital stability and even for the viability of society itself. Durkheim (1960) argued for sexual division of labour as an example of organic solidarity.

Let's take the case of Mumbai dance bars to understand the dilemma and dialectics. The Supreme Court gave its verdict on favour of reopening the dance bars (dna, July 16, 2013). Deciding on the constitutionality of the ban on dance performances under the Bombay Police (Amendment) Act of 2005, the apex court upheld the Bombay HC order in favour of dance bars in Mumbai. The apex court recently reiterated the same judgment in lifting the ban on dance bars once again by the Maharashtra Government (The Times of India, October 15, 2015). This may be a judgment in favour of the rights guaranteed in the Constitution, but is there any real empowerment of women taking place? The plight of this profession is depicted by Faleiro (2010) from the very journalistic perspective. There are conflicts among different organs of the state namely the legislature that bans the dance bars; the executive that imposes the law by banning dance in bars, and the court that sets aside the ban being unconstitutional. Society is the stake holder but divided with divergent arguments. It can be understood whether it's the freedom of food or freedom of dignity, or it can be understood as the freedom of choice. The larger question is whether it the choice of empowerment. What is clear is that the feminist movement cannot be independent of the socio-economy of the country.

Two pictures emerge in this context. The common picture is the humiliating gender discrimination and violence. Amidst this common one, some individuals emerge being very powerful like Durga or Kali. However, they do not change the course of history but enjoy power in the same society known to be hostile to women. They can be captured from the action perspective in which social actors rather than social structure grow and capture cultural capital, economic capital, or political capital. Bourdieu's habituate can be helpful to understand this. As India is heading towards knowledge economy, the growing (professional) education of women creates space for their own empowerment and subsequent changes are taking pale in the interactive patterns at micro level. Can it be said that a powerful lady in public space won't get subjected to domestic violence or sexual harassment at home or at workplace? In the recent past, there were allegations of sexual impropriety even in judiciary including the Supreme Court.

Comte's juxtaposition of women liberates the Victorian dichotomy between women as angels (meekly self-sacrificial) or (sexualised) demons (Ray: 1999). Women would thus be liberated into a romanticized asexual space defined by the intersecting dichotomies between society and nature, public and private, egoism and altruism, intellect and emotion, desire and purity (ibid). Comte's assumptions are far from reality.

Phenomenological Empowerment: Some Observations

The Calendar Girls traces the story of five models who rise to fame after featuring in a calendar but then fate plays a terrible game with them. Many celebrated models in public life expose their bodies for commercial advertisements or films. Many are known to be porn stars or item girls. After all, they are glamorous and powerful in public life. There is a society that makes it possible for a few women to construct their own reality and become powerful. This affects the value system of the society and diminishes society's regard for women. LeMoncheck (1985) is critical of these dehumanizing women who set out to define sex objectification and explains why it is often morally objectionable and consider ways of reducing the incidence of its occurrence.

One study comparing images of women in weekly U.S. news magazines (*Time* and *Life*) to weekly Indian magazines (*India Today* and *Illustrated Weekly* of India) found very similar portrayals of women in subordinate or accessory poses among these four magazines (Griffin, Viswanath, & Schwartz, 1994). The authors concluded that many of the western advertising conventions and poses for women were being transferred cross-culturally in conjunction with concepts like professionalism by western multinational advertising agencies. In certain areas, such as the portrayal of women in predominately housewife or domestic management settings, Indian magazines far outstripped their U.S. counterparts. When comparing the use of sexual pursuit as a theme in advertisements (men pursuing women in an overtly sexual way), however, U.S. magazines used these portrayals three times more often than Indian magazines. Despite being a men's fragrance,

Tom Ford for Men campaigns show nude women in erotic poses with the product strategically placed. Do such phenomenological advertisements empower women? Sociology does not go by any single perspective. Structural theories may deny, but action theorists may confirm. Hall (1997) illustrates, the concept of shared meanings places its emphasis on cultural practices. It is participants in a culture who give meaning to people, objects and events. Since things in themselves rarely have any single and fixed meaning, they need to be given meanings by participants of the culture concerned. He also suggests that members of the same culture must share sets of concepts, images and ideas which enable them to think and feel about the world, and thus to interpret the world in roughly similar ways.

In the picture, the models are glamorous and charismatic in society, but in picture, the pose themselves inferior to shoes. This phenomenological empowerment appears to be possible outside social structure. Just to put it in juxtaposition, the Supreme Court observation is that a woman's body is her temple (The Times of India, July 1, 2015).

What makes empowerment possible?

It's the placement at organisational structure. It is linking biography to history. The driver of a minister is more powerful than that of a doctor. It's the proximity to power. India right now has four women Chief Ministers, a few Governors, a good number of ministers, bureaucrats, judgers, advocates, etc. They are powerful in public domain. Going beyond the stereotype structural functional paradigm, let's understand empowerment from other perspectives. Empowerment is a multi-faceted, multidimensional and multi-layered concept. Women's empowerment is a process in which women gain greater share of control over resources material, human and intellectual like knowledge, information, ideas and financial resources like money and access to decision-making at home, community, society and nation to gain power. According to the Country Report of Government of India (2001), Empowerment means moving from a position of enforced powerlessness to one of power. Therefore, the empowerment of women or gender (dis)parity is not independent of class / caste. It appears that the upper and the lower strata do not care for the value system as much as the middle class do. For the middle class, functionalism wherein institutions dominate the individuals may be the befitting perspective, but for the upper strata, the action perspective wherein individuals defines their own acts. Feminism has its own arguments. Classical Marxism considered family in terms of private property and advocated its abolition.

The concept of power is as old as the birth of Political Science which is defined as the shaping and sharing of power. In sociology, postmodernity underlines the role of power to develop its literature. The overwhelming euphoria of women empowerment strongly suggests the prevalence of postmodernism in globalised India. Modernity is defensive. Even change is also within the prescribed schemes as Parson puts in AGIL. Therefore, what is anomic (Durkheim) is also structural (Merton). With the flexibility of macro structure, there is space for micro structures to grow relatively independently and then get linked to network available on social media, otherwise, global media. The epistemology of post-modernism stands opposite to the meta-narratives imposed. The construction of social reality on the empowerment of women is viral on social media. Therefore, it can be called a mediated empowerment of women. Here lies the actual challenge.

Feminism is not the mainstream discourse even in urban India. Therefore, what the educated urban women are struggling is their right to be equally treated which receives adverse response in the family system and gets reflected in the domestic violence. What came latest in defence of patriarchy is the claim made by a Chhattisgarh school textbook that the working women are responsible for unemployment (The Times of India, Sept. 22, 2015).

The single denomination that can define human relation is the allocation of power embodied in the institutional framework. Therefore, the empowerment of women has to be understood from the position of women in the power structure. Therefore, the scope for empowerment at home is limited especially between husband and wife in traditional societies. Let's consider a case that can reveal the internal dynamics of the organisational structure pertaining to women empowerment. The lady running a brothel is found to be the most powerful one in the organisation. The others have little rights but to surrender. The motherin-law in the household is the most powerful one. What makes it possible? The organisation structure and behaviour (the usual interactive practices) makes it possible. It would be wrong to assume gender gap in terms of conflicts of opposite genders. The same gender is also in the conflicting mode. Therefore, the debate over women empowerment is more of organisational and less of gender. The larger issue stands between the constitutional and legal provisions of women empowerment on one hand and the patriarchal social issues on the other. The state is as young as sixty seven, and the society is as old as five thousand years. This young state marked with rational legal authority seems to be too small before the old society marked with traditional authority. There is sharp contrast between the old society and the new state.

Therefore, the constitutional provisions for women empowerment do not work in social context. The state is secular but the society is marked with the contours of religions. There is upsurge of religious activities even amidst technology loaded digital India. Therefore, it's about the interfaces of authorities. In parliamentary forms of democracy, as in India, the government (i.e., rational legal authority) belongs to the party that mostly represent the society (i.e., traditional authority). This has also affected the process of women empowerment.

To what extent can women grow? The sociological answer to this question would be to the extent society permits. Here society is manifested in three different forms—institutional, organisational, and interactive. Even men can't grow beyond institutional limits. However, the organisational framework provides flexibility and the same institution, for example, family, can have different organisational practice. Under family as institution which is common to a large section of society, the organisational family is different to different individual family. This is also different at interactive level. However, there is little change in the hegemony. To the Tamil Magazine, *Kumudam Reporter*, women who wear leggings deserve to be shamed (Huff Post India: September 24, 2015).

An Observation

Let's conclude with a remark by the CARE's Director in Burundi. It reflects the real dilemma and dialectics of the empowerment of women:

> If we're going to talk about women's empowerment, we have to talk about the problem of sexual violence. It's great if the head of the community development committee is a woman. But if she's going home and getting raped every night by her brother-in-law, is she empowered? No. (McIlvaine 2005).

References

Alam, Jayanti. 2013. *Religion, Patriarchy and Capitalism*. Delhi: Kalpaz Publications.

Barker, E. 1951. *Principles of Social and Political Theory*: Oxford: Clarendon Press.

Becker, Gary S. 1981. *A Treatise on the Family*. Cambridge, Mass: Harvard University Press.

Berger, P. 1963. *Invitation to Sociology: A Humanistic Perspective.* New York: Anchor Books.

Business Today, magazine, August 31, 2014.

Bourdieu, P. (1998). La domination masculine [Male domination]. Edition du Seuil.

dna, daily, July 16, 2013

Durkheim, Emile. 1960 [1893: 60-61]. *The Division of Labour in Society* Glencoe, Ill.: The Free Press.

Faleiro, Sonia. 2010. *Beautiful Thing*. New Delhi: Penguin.

Giddens. 1984. *Constitution of Society Outline of the Theory of Structuration* Cambridge: Polity Press.

_______. 2006. *Sociology*. Cambridge: Polity Press.

Goffman, E. (1977). The arrangement between the sexes. *Theory and Society, 4*, 301-331.

Griffin, M., Viswanath, K., & Schwartz, D. 1994. Gender advertising in the U.S. and India: Exporting cultural stereotypes. *Media, Culture & Society*, 16, 487–507.

Government of India 2001. The National Policy for the Empowerment of Women 2001, Department of Women and Child Development, Ministry of Human Resource Development, New Delhi, 2001.

Hall, Stuart (Ed). 1997. The work of representation', in *Representations: Cultural Representation and Signifying Practice*. New Delhi: Sage.

HuffPost India June 29, 2015

HuffPost India: September 24, 2015

LeMoncheck, Linda (1985) *Dehumanizing Women: Treating Persons as Sex Objects*. Totowa, NJ.

Marx, Karl. 1875/1970. Critique of the Gotha Programme,' in *Marx/Engels Selected Works,* Volume Three, p. 1330; Moscow: Progress Publishers.

McIlvaine, Kassie CARE's Director in Burundi

Source: 'We are also Human:' Identity and Power in Gender Relations; Drinkwater, M., CARE 2005.

Mumbai Mirror, May 20, 2015

NABARD: Circular No: 65(A)/ MCID-04 / 2011-12

Parsons, Talcott. 1949. The social structure of the family', in *The Family: Its Function and Destiny*, ed. Ruth Anshen. New York: Harper and Brothers, pp. 173-201.

Ray, Larry J. 1999. *Theorizing Classical Sociology*. Philadelphia: Open University Press.

Sen, S. 2004. A Report on Trafficking in Women and Children in India 2002-2003. New Delhi: National Human Rights Commission, UNIFEM, Institute of Social Science.

The Deccan Chronicle, December 17, 2013

The Hindu, daily, November 11, 2014

The Hindu, daily, November 30, 2014

The Hindu, daily, January 1, 2015

The Hindu, daily, March 14, 2015

The Hindu, daily, March 18, 2014

The Hindu, daily, March 25, 2014

The Hindu, daily, June 15, 2015

The Hindu, daily, July 6, 2015

The Hindu, daily, September 6, 2014

The Hindu, daily, September 24, 2015

The Hindu, daily, October 17, 2015

The Hindu Centre for Politics and Public Policy: June 15, 2015

The Indian Express, daily, April 11, 2014

The Indian Express, daily, August 9, 2015

The New Indian Express, daily, January 25, 2014

The Times of India, daily, November 5, 2009

The Times of India, daily, August 24, 2014
The Times of India, daily, October 27, 2014
The Times of India, daily, December 31, 2014
The Times of India, daily, May 14, 2015
The Times of India, daily, May 21, 2015
The Times of India, daily, July 1, 2015
The Times of India, daily, Sept. 21, 2015
The Times of India, daily, Sept. 22, 2015
The Times of India, daily, October 15, 2015

Website Citations

1. http 1. *www.wadinet.de*
2. http 2. (https://www.amnestyusa.org/our-work/issues/women-s-rights/violenceagainst-women/violence-against-women-information)
3. http 3. http://ips.stanford.edu/)
4. http 4. www.wca.nic.in

4

Using Reading as a Resource to Help Dalit Students Learn English and Achieve their Desired Socio-economic Status

— Govindaiah Godavarthi

Introduction

> *Mahatmas have come and Mahatmas have gone but untouchables in* India have remained as untouchables. **— B.R. Ambedkar**

After the mother tongue, English is the only language that is more important than any other for Dalit students to sustain in a world of cutthroat competition and to obtain a respectable position in society, especially in the Indian society. The elite and caste Hindus, upper castes, progress using English while Dalits lag behind to learn and use this language due to lack of knowledge in English, inferiority complex and presuming English being elite Language.

Without English, upliftment of Dalits is almost impossible. We see that the world is changing rapidly and if we want to be a part of global citizenship then English is one of the tools that will help us to develop in all spheres of life.

The sweeping changes that have come by way of increased industrialisation, massive economic restructuring and the new demands made in terms of job requirements. Liberalisation, Privatisation and Globalisation, have made it highly essential for imparting instruction in English. English has come to occupy the first place in terms of importance and the number of users. It is to the fortunate advantage of Indians that English is taught and learnt as a second language, and the importance of learning English as a second language, can hardly be over-looked.

Facts and figures regarding Dalits

According to the Socio-Economic and Caste Census 2011, 38 per cent SC community lives BPL. 43 per cent own permanent homes. 17.7 per cent own permanent homes in rural areas. Less than one per cent of the SC community in rural areas had a member earning more than ₹ 10,000 a month.

Socio-economic enablement of the Dalits for Education

I quote Mahatma Jyotirao Phule, a well-known social reformer of the nineteenth century, worked ceaselessly for education of the women and the Dalits, and reform the Indian social structure. He says, *Without education mind is lost, Without mind morality is lost, Without morality mobility is lost, Without mobility economy is lost, Without economy shudras were degraded....*

Across India, it is socio-economic problems of the Dalit students which makes them deprived of common resources of the country. So this depravity is because of lack of awareness, education and proper guidance. In this regard, English language education can help them to attain the desired socio-economic status.

The role of Lord Macaulay in Empowering the Dalits

B. R. Ambedkar, the leader and patron saint of the Dalits, knew that without English education he would not be able to fight with upper class. He rightly pointed out that *English was* the *milk of lioness, and it was necessary for every Dalit.*

It is due to Lord Macaulay's English language policy – right or wrong – in India, the Dalits were attracted towards this new international language. Though it was a commodity of the elite and Brahmins initially and difficult to learn, many students of the marginalised have attained proficiency to take up jobs in the Departments of English and Linguistics and improved his/her self-esteem in a society dominated by Brahmin ideology.

Mere slogans or sloganeering does not change the fate of Dalits. They have to shrug off all their fears and come out of their inferiority complex to work shoulder to shoulder with those who were not looking down upon them. We have to remember that only modern English education that will make the society caste free. It is the only tool which will help them come out of socio-economic and political depravity.

In this context, what can we do in order to make the learning of English easier and effective? The content given below is a study on the students of Andhra and Telangana social welfare residential schools, which puts forth a proposition that reading helps the Dalits, to learn English faster.

Importance of English in India

Today it is no longer a wise proposition to look upon this language as colonial baggage. English is now an indispensable instrument necessary for the socio-economic development of the country. It is needed if India is to stake a claim to being one of the rapidly developing nations of the world.

English occupies a prominent place among the languages used in India for several reasons. It is a library language and much of the literature pertaining to developments in science and communication, arts, social sciences, philosophy etc are reported in English. It is "recognised as an essential component of formal education, and as the preferred medium of learning, with specialised education, and as the preferred medium of education; socially it is recognised and upheld as a mark of education, culture, and prestige. The polity and society confer great value on the learning of English knowing bi-multi-linguals. Gupta R.S. and Kapil Kapoor, (1991:19)

The dictates of time have ensured the all-time popularity of this language. The IT industry alone generates revenues worth several billion dollars per annum. The call-center, institutes training students for

GMAT, TOFEL, and IELTS, multinational companies that recruit engineers, content writers, programmers etc., on stupendous salaries, all of these generate money worth billions of dollars. Ironically, Indian teachers of English are now in large numbers in England, USA and Canada teaching English to native speakers'. Indian students find that the language of higher education is English.

English continues to act as a link language and promises job prospects for anyone who has a fairly good command over it. Thus, the pivotal role English has played in shaping the destiny and future of India is indeed a point worth noting for those who argue in support of instruction in the mother tongue.

English was introduced as one of the languages under the three-language formula. The central schools run by the central government, the Novodaya Vidyalayas and the army schools as well as schools following CBSE syllabus have English as a second language. Regional medium schools have English as one of the languages.

In AP, the three-language formula applies to state schools under private management. In govt. run schools English is taught as a second language though students are taught subjects in Telugu. The present study has its focus on the Andhra Pradesh State Social Welfare Residential Educational Institutions Society schools (APSWREIS). These are schools that are meant for children from rural areas who have little or no access to many of the facilities that are available to their counterparts in the city.

AP and Telangana State Social Welfare Residential Educational Institutions Society schools (TSSWREIS) schools are residential schools run by the state government for the benefit of the children of the poor and the under-privileged. These schools have classes from I-X and Junior colleges. The teachers teach students in Telugu and English is also taught through the mother tongue. As the students are drawn from economically backward sections, the facilities they enjoy and the support they get from home is minimal. Therefore, most students struggle to cope with the language, and the subjects in school. Learners are rather poor at spelling, vocabulary, reading, and grammar, in short, all aspects of language. It was also noticed that the students were willing to learn provided they had a source to rely on and help them out in times of difficulty.

The context of the study

A brief description of the school selected for the study is presented below. The present study focused on the learners of Andhra Pradesh and Telanagana Social Welfare Residential Educational Institutes Society School. It is an AP and TS government society management school. It follows the state syllabus. The school is managed well with highly qualified, experienced, and trained teachers. The classrooms are spacious enough to seat 35 to 40 students per class. They are well ventilated and provided with the basic infrastructural facilities.

Students are quiet, well disciplined, and regular to class. They are highly motivated to learn something every day, especially in English. However, what is learnt in class is not practiced because they do not have enough exposure. English unfortunately, is often taught through the mother tongue and whatever English learners hear is only from the teacher. They are accustomed to listening to all their lessons through translation method; they could not cope with the writing tasks in the *Second language*. They, however, made great efforts in this direction. Students write confidently using the *First language*, they have excellent word power and ideas. There is no regular practice or habit of writing small texts, initiated by the teacher. Students have creative ideas but lack teacher-support or encouragement in writing tasks.

Reading as a tool to improve English

The paper bases itself on WLA to language acquisition by using reading as a main resource; some arguments related to teaching of reading are discussed in the following section.

Good reading habits are to be developed right from the beginning in schools. Somehow, some teachers are always able to encourage the children to develop their reading skills, while most others fail. Teaching reading has been a failure in most cases. Reading has been neglected in most schools and teachers think that after children have been taught to read letters of the alphabet, words and short sentences, their part of the job is over, and the children are left to themselves to develop the skills of reading and comprehension.

John Ruskin's observation: "Books are the best of friends—they are never too busy for you" is apt for all ages and it applies more so to school college students, who have simply forgotten the act of reading. It is also often understood that students of high schools and colleges are supposed to read only the class books and are never required to read general books. It is absolutely wrong to think that it is undesirable to read anything other than the class textbooks. Perhaps it is essential at this particular age to read other literatures also, to improve one's vocabulary, or to gain general knowledge.

Conclusion

The teacher needs to adapt his/her techniques to the proficiency level of students. The English teacher therefore needs to understand and empathise with the anxiety faced by students who move from the mother tongue and other known languages to learning the new language in rural setting, while tackling intelligently the boredom that can creep into the elementary level of language teaching in urban and semi-urban setting. This sensitisation process is done mainly through teacher development.

SWAEROES TEN COMMANDMENTS OR PROMISES?

The new set of commandments

1. Thou shall be righteous
2. Thou art not inferior to anyone
3. Thou shall be a noble leader
4. Thou shall think big and aim high
5. Thou shall do what you love but be different
6. Thou shall not give up
7. Thou shall not blame others for your failures
8. Thou shall respect yourself
9. Thou shall repay what you borrow
10. Thou shall not fear the unknown

5

Access to Education and Health Among Social Groups: A Case Study of Migrant Slum Households of Gadag-Betageri City in Karnataka State

— B.H. Nagoor

I. Introduction

The very low economic base, lack of education and ignorance of the migrated labour households in cities, make them deprived of basic necessities of life and they lead distressful and unsecured life. This segment of urban population is excluded from the mainstream of society. Such migrated labourers are mainly engaged in urban informal sector and the quality of work available for these labourers is very low. Such labour migrants, in search of work in cities often end up with a precarious livelihood, low income, typically the hallmarks of the low end of the urban informal sector. This manifested in increasing slums and ghettoes in cities.

In this backdrop, the thrust of the present study is to highlight the nature of deprivation, with reference to health and education among social groups. Examine the policy response in addressing education and health needs. The important aim of study would be to generate not only a set of policy recommendations, but also define the institutional frame work through which such policies can be meaningfully implemented. The study of problems of migrated labourers in cities is not new, the earlier studies however, do not focus on nature of deprivation of such labour households and problems in accessing the various government programmes meant for such labour households.

As part of larger study on selected cities of Karnataka, the present study mainly focuses on Gadag-Betigeri city. According to census 2001, in Karnataka state, Gadag –Betigeri city witnessed second highest inmigration during 1991 to 2001 in proportion to the total population of the city.

II. Methodology of the Study

The study has been conducted for migrated labour households, staying in various slums and other public places of Gadag-Betigeri city. A sample of 300 labour households spread over in 29 slums have been surveyed.

The age of slums varies from one slum to another slum. There are slums with more than 40 years of old and there are slums with less than four years. There is noticeable difference between old and new slums. The physical environment of all the surveyed slums is unhygienic and varies from one slum to another slum. However, compared to new slums, the households' living condition in old slums is better.

The migrated labour households' survey has been carried out by the research scholars of Department of Economics, Karnataka University, Dharwad. The labourers who have been migrated during last 15 years are considered for the study. The study covers the entire Gadag-Betigeri city. Looking at the homogeneity in the living conditions of migrated labour households of Gadag-Betigeri city, sample labour households have been selected randomly. From the randomly selected migrated labour households, categorisation has been made on the basis of caste, religion, gender, occupation, age group, place of origin, income, and level of education. The purpose of such categorisation of the households is to understand the living conditions of the various groups and the accessibility of such households in benefiting various programmes meant for the urban deprived. And, also to identify the discrepancy in utilising the government programmes among migrated households. By doing so, the study aims for identifying lacuna in existing public policy in improving the living conditions of migrated labour households staying in urban slums and need for appropriate policy formulation if any. By analysing the existing various government programmes and social security measures, the study also makes the suggestions, which may be incorporated for better utilisation of the government programmes meant for vulnerable and deprived. Various information pertaining to study has been collected from the labour households through design questionnaire and direct interview. As part of the study we interacted with NGO working for urban deprived. The study is divided into five sections. The third section deals with access to education and health among migrant slum households. On the basis of findings of the study, the policy suggestions have been made in the fourth section.

III Access to Education and Health among migrant slum households

In market oriented economy, it is very important on the part of the state to provide minimum level of education and health facility to everyone, otherwise vulnerable and underprivileged poor will be left out from development process, thereby leading to large inequality and social disharmony in the society. Recognising this, the state, since independence has been putting its efforts to make education and health facility affordable to everyone, still many are deprived of access to education and health. How to provide minimum level of education and good health facility to every one? What are the deficits in implementation of government health and educational schemes? Is there any problem with implementation mechanism of such schemes? What are the alternatives to implementation mechanism? These are the basic questions the study is trying to address.

III.1 Education among migrant slum households

This section deals with education among migrant households. The education pattern of all surveyed migrants belongs to above the six years age reveal that 46 per cent were illiterate, 23 per cent were just literate, 18 per cent had education up to class V, 13 per cent had education ranging from class V to PUC and there were five graduates, representing less than one per cent (Fig. 1).

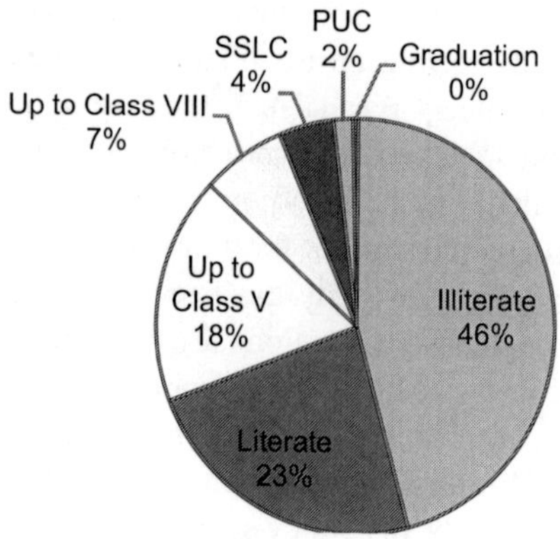

Source: Calculated from field Survey.

Fig. 1: Education level of migrant slum households.

We also worked out the education level of young population belongs to age group between 18 and 30 years (Fig. 2) to see the potentiality of migrants for skill training. This population represents 33 per cent of the surveyed migrants. We find that 42 per cent were illiterate, 49 per cent were literate with some formal schooling of 1-3 years, and 9 per cent had education up to class V.

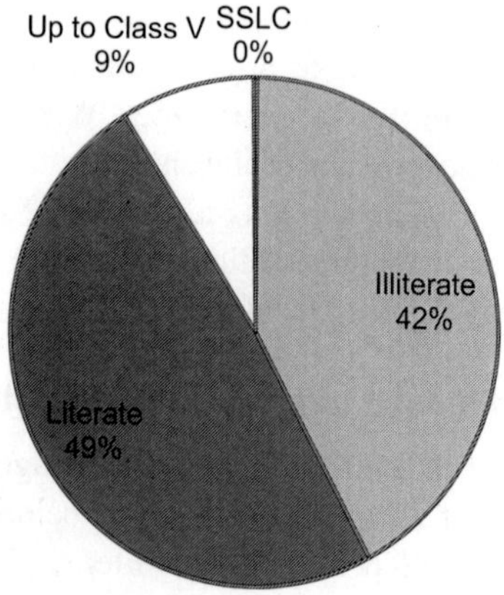

Source: Calculated from field Survey.

Fig. 2: Education level of migrant slum households belongs to the age group between 18-30 years.

Education level of migrants' children belongs to age group 6-14 years

Discussion on level of education of the migrants reveals that the low educated migrant workers, with no economic assets, are working in unsecured and low paid informal sector. With such status, what they can offer for their children, especially education. Education plays an important role in the earning capacity of an individual. For complete improvement of such underprivileged households and to bring such households to mainstream economic development, education for children of migrants is very essential. In this sub-section, education level of migrants' children belongs to age group 6-14 years has been discussed. Of this surveyed migrant population, 20 per cent belongs to the age group between 6-14 years. Information on education level of such children (Fig. 3) show that 4 per cent are illiterate and never had any exposure of formal schooling. 80 per cent had education up to primary level and had the exposure of formal schooling. 16 per cent of children had education up to secondary level.

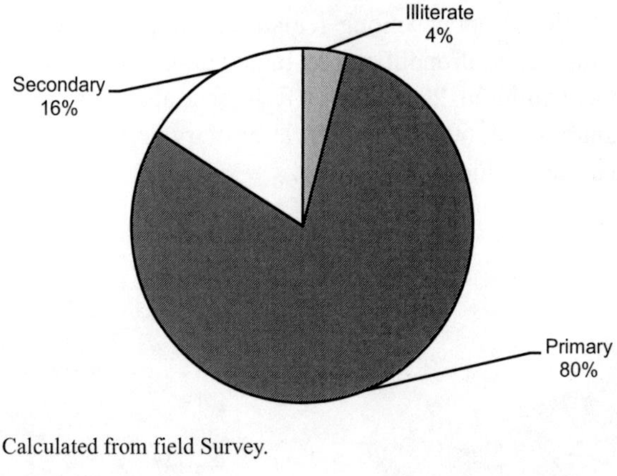

Source: Calculated from field Survey.

Fig. 3: Education level among slum children between the age 6-14 years.

Information on education level among male and female children (Fig. 4 and 5) shows that male children are more illiterate than female children. And, more female children had education up to secondary level than the male children in the same category.

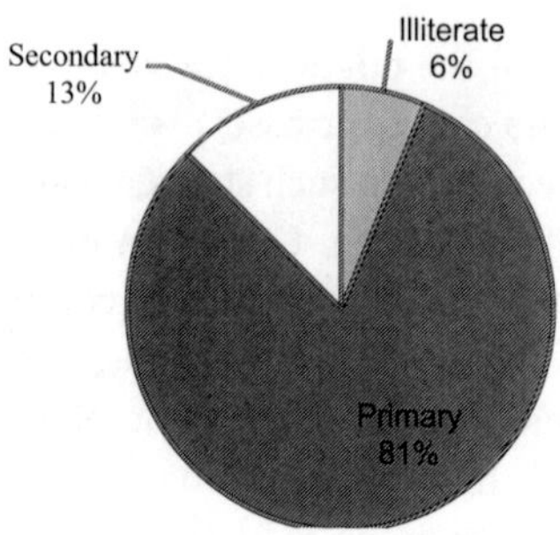

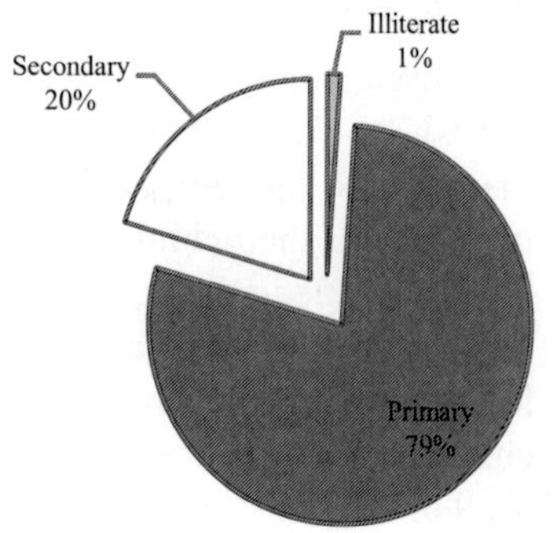

Source: Calculated from field Survey.

Fig. 4: Education level among male children.

Fig. 5: Education level among female children.

The school dropout among the children in the age group 6-14 years, it is 17.41 per cent (Fig. 7). The dropout among the male and female children in the age group 6-14 years has also been calculated in Fig. 8. It reveals that dropout among female children is very high (33 per cent) compared to dropout among male children (6 per cent). Among the dropout children, 20 per cent left the school at very early, i.e. at the pre-primary level, 60 per cent left at primary level and 20 per cent at secondary level (Fig. 6).

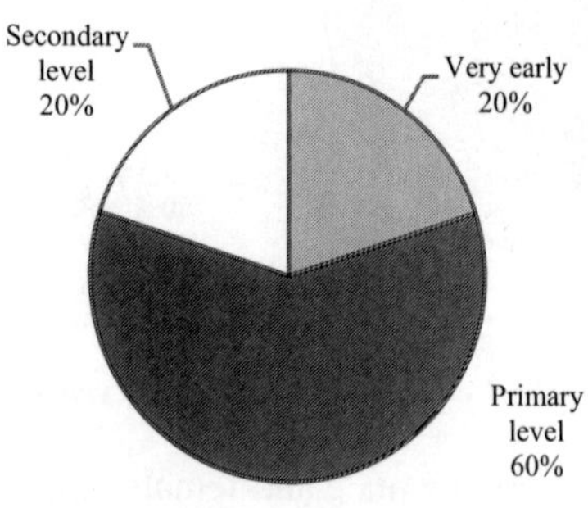

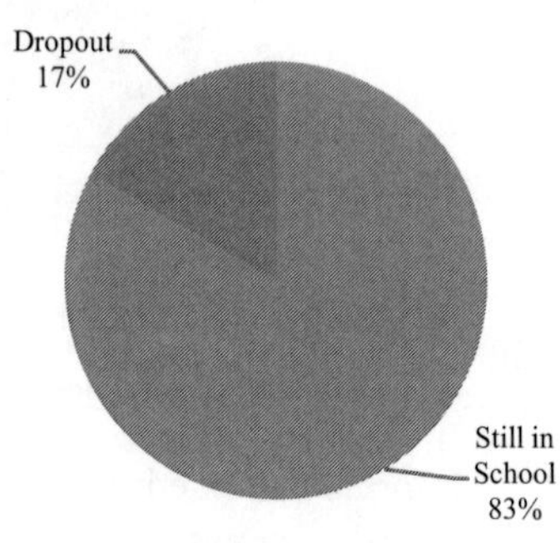

Source: Calculated from field Survey.

Fig. 6: When children dropout?

Fig. 7: Dropout among school going children.

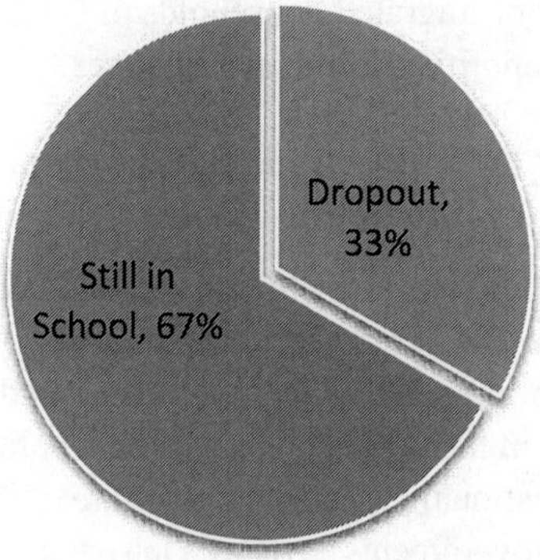

Source: Calculated from field Survey.

Fig. 8: Dropout among female children.

The discussion on education level among migrant children reveal that, the education level of migrants' children is very low and not enough to get secured and comfortably paid employment. Though, in case of Gadag-Betigeri slums, children belongs to the age group 6-14 years, 96 per cent are literature and had some years of formal schooling and some had education up to secondary level, their learning ability is very low. In competitive organised sector, it is very difficult for such children to compete with other children and secure the job. Only alternative will be to work in low paid informal and unorganised sector. This indicates that there is no better future for children of migrants.

Access to Educational Benefits

To provide education for everyone, government has introduced number of schemes. Government of India educational policy emphasis that education must play a positive and interventionist role in correcting social and regional imbalance, empowering women, and in securing a rightful place for the disadvantaged and the minorities. Government is firmly committed to providing education for all, the priority areas being free and compulsory elementary education, covering children with special needs, eradication of illiteracy, education for women's equality, and special focus on the education of SCs/STs and Minorities. In this section, the study looked at how the educational benefits have reached the children of poor migrated households of Gadag –Betigeri city and reasons for not benefiting from such schemes.

Scholarship to (SC/ST) child, Balika Samrudhi Yojana and Mid-day meal, Uniforms and Books

The migrated labour households' access to education is captured in Table -1 From the previous discussion, we find that from every 10 children, 2 children are dropout. Tables 1 and 2, reveals that, the children who are in the school are not fully benefited from the various government educational schemes. For welfare of SC/ST children, both central and state governments have been introducing various scholarship (financial support) schemes. Though, the schemes are applicable to all SC/ST children, the findings of field level study show that, 50 per cent of eligible beneficiaries are not benefited. This shows that, still large number of SC/ST children are not benefiting from such schemes. Among non-beneficiary households, 61 per cent are not aware of welfare schemes for SC/ST children, 24 per cent of eligible households have not benefited as they frequently shift from one place to another place.

In the case of scholarship to SC/ST children, only 50 per cent are benefited. In case of Balika Samrudhi Yojana, only 12.4 per cent are benefited. However, in the case of Mid-day meal, free uniform and books, around 80 to 90 per cent are benefited. In human development literature, prime importance is given to access to education for human empowerment and uplifting the poor. Though, we find number of programmes initiated by the central and Karnataka state governments to provide education to everyone, still many underprivileged are deprived of education and government educational benefit schemes. What are the reasons for not benefiting from such schemes? How to make these schemes effective and provide education to every one? These questions are discussed in the subsequent section.

The study also looked at existence of discrimination among social groups in benefiting the government welfare schemes. This is captured in Tables 1 and 2. We find that, in the case of Scholarship to (SC/ST) children, ST households are benefited more than that of SC households. However, in the case of Balika Samrudhi Yojana, Mid-day meal, free

Table 1: Access to educational benefits of migrated households (Scholarship to (SC/ST) child, Balika Samrudhi Yojana and Mid-day meal)

Religion	*Scholarship to (SC/ST) child*			*Balika Samrudhi Yojana*			*Mid-day meal*		
	Bene-fited	*Not Benefited*	*Not Applicable*	*Bene-fited*	*Not Benefited*	*Not Applicable*	*Bene-fited*	*Not Benefited*	*Not Applicable*
Hindu	50	49	17	12(14.29)	84	135	111(91)	11	109
SC	43(49.4)	44	16	12(27.27)	44	47	56(91.8)	5	42
ST	07(58.3)	05	01	0	4	9	6(100)	0	7
OBC	-	-	-	0	33	75	46(90.2)	5	57
Others	-	-	-	0	3	4	3(75)	1	3
Muslims	-	-	-	3(16.67)	18	39	32(88.9)	4	24
Christian	-	-	-	0	3	3	3(75)	1	2
Others	-	-	-	0	1	2	0	1	2
All	50(50.5)	49(49.5)	17	15(12.4)	106(87.6)	179	146(89.6)	17(10.4)	137

Source: Author calculation from household survey.

Note: Figures in the brackets shows percentage share in total applicable households.

books and uniform schemes, SC households are benefited more than that of any other social groups considered for the study. What emerges from this is that, there is no discrimination for SC households in benefiting from the government programmes such as Balika Samrudhi Yojana, Mid-day meal, free books and uniform schemes. In fact, in majority cases, SC households are benefited more than that of other social groups.

Table 2: Access to educational benefits of migrated households (Free uniforms and books for the children)

Religion	*Uniforms*			*Books*		
	Benefited	*Not Benefited*	*Not Applicable*	*Benefited*	*Not Benefited*	*Not Applicable*
Hindu	97 (81.5)	22	112	97 (79.5)	25	109
SC	49 (83)	10	44	51 (86.4)	8	44
ST	6 (100)	0	7	6 (100)	0	7
OBC	38 (77.5)	11	59	36 (69.2)	16	56
Others	4 (80)	1	2	4 (80)	1	2
Muslims	32 (89)	4	24	31 (83.8)	6	23
Christian	3 (75)	1	2	3 (75)	1	2
Others	0	1	2	0	1	2
All	132 (82.5)	28 (17.5)	140	131 (79.9)	33 (20.1)	136

Source: Author calculation from household survey.

Note: Figures in the brackets shows percentage share in total applicable households.

III.2 Health status of migrated households

From the field survey of 300 labour households, which are reported in Table 3, we find that, some people suffer from chronic illnesses like Tuberculosis, Cholera, Diabetes, Dengue, etc. The study is interested in whether they have received any treatment or not, where they have received the treatment and reasons for not receiving the treatment in government hospitals. It is evident from the respondents that all diseased people have received the treatment. Though, the proportionate share of receiving treatment in public hospital is high, however, 20-30 per cent diseased people received treatment in private hospitals.

This shows inability of public hospitals in providing services to all chronically diseased poor people. It will be expensive for poor households to receive treatment in private hospitals. Such health expenditure will affect the poor households' livelihood.

The health profile of the female migrated household members (Table 4) reveals that, during pregnancy and at the time of delivery, in majority cases (97-100 per cent), females received the treatment in hospitals. There are cases (7-9 per cent), where female received treatment in private hospitals also. During the migrated households' survey, respondents revealed that public health workers are playing important role in creating health awareness among pregnant women and also providing free medicine during pregnancy.

Table 3: General health profile of the migrated household members

Type of Diseases	*Number of people suffering from illness*	*Number of people received Treatment**		*Place of treatment***		
		Yes	*No*	*Public*	*Private*	*Home*
Chronic Illness (Diabetes, BP, back-pain)	20	20 (100)		16 (80)	4 (20)	0
Chronic Cough	3	3 (100)		2 (67)	1 (33)	0
Tuberculosis	6	6 (100)		6 (100)	0	0
Cholera	4	4 (100)		4 (100)	0	0
Any fever (Dengue, Viral, Chickenguniya, Measles, Mumps)	18	18 (100)		14 (77.8)	4 (22.2)	0

Source: Author calculation from household survey.

Note: * Figures in the brackets shows percentage share of treatment received by the diseased people in total diseased people.

** Figures in the brackets shows percentage share of treatment received by the diseased people in public and private hospital.

Another observation from 300 labour households' survey is that, only three per cent of population is in the age group of 60 years and above. This is quite lower compared to national average of 6.97 per cent during 2001 and predicted 8.94 per cent during 2011. And there are 56 widows. This shows early deaths, especially male deaths. We also looked at reasons for not using public hospitals for treatment by the diseased people (Table 5). We find that, majority of respondents, who have taken treatment in private hospitals said that, public hospitals are too far away from their place of stay. Few respondents also said that, timings of the public hospitals do not suit them and they have problem in trusting the behaviour of the staff.

Table 4: Health profile of the female migrated household members

	Number of female suffering from illness	*Number of people received Treatment**		*Place of treatment***		
		Yes	*No*	*Public*	*Private*	*Home*
Uterus, breasts, cervix related diseases	1	1 (100)		1 (100)	0	0
Delivery in last five years	101	98 (97.3)	03 (2.7)	92 (91)	09 (9)	0
Pregnant lady medical treatment (Vitamin tablets, Doses of TT, Milk bread, Tests of HIV)	138	135 (97.8)	03 (2.2)	128 (92.8)	09 (6.5)	1 (.7)

Source: Author calculation from household survey.

Note: * Figures in the brackets shows percentage share of treatment received by the diseased people in total diseased people.

** Figures in the brackets shows percentage share of treatment received by the diseased people in public and private hospital.

Table 5: Reasons for not using public hospital during sickness by the migrated labour households

Type of Diseases	*Facility too far*	*Facility not open*	*Timings does not suit*	*Not trust*	*Cost is same*	*Behaviour of the health staff*
Chronic Illness (Diabetes, BP, back-pain)	14	0	2	3	0	1
Chronic Cough	1	0	0	1	0	1
Tuberculosis						
Cholera						
Any fever (Dengue, Viral, Chickenguniya, Measles, Mumps)	1	0	4	1	0	0
Any female related (Uterus, breasts, cervix)						
During delivery	6	0	3	2	0	1
During pregnancy (Vitamin tablets, Doses of TT, Milk bread, Tests of HIV)	7	0	1	3	0	2

Source: Author calculation from household survey.

Note: Figure shows number of households.

Access to health benefits of migrated households

From time to time, government initiated good number of health benefit programmes for urban underprivileged. It is important to know how much these programmes have benefited. The effectiveness of some of the important health related programme in reaching the poor migrated households has been discussed in this section. It is interesting to note that, the proportionate share of benefited households is very low in many health related programme (Table 6). In the case of Yashaswini/ any other health card the benefited households' percentage share is less than five per cent. The special nutrition programme (Vitamin A for less than five years) and Girl child benefits should have benefited all eligible beneficiaries. However, the proportionate share of beneficiaries is 26 and 29 per cent respectively. The TB Programme (DOTS) benefited households' percentage share is 33.33 per cent, what emerges from this analysis is but failure of health programmes in reaching all eligible beneficiaries.

Table 6: Access to health benefits of migrated households

Immunisation	*Percentage share of immunisation*
BCG	97.6
POLIO 1	98.4
POLIO 2	99.2
POLIO 3	98.8
DPT 1	98.8
DPT 2	98.8
DPT 3	98.8
Measles	95.6

Source: Author calculation from household survey.

Child immunisation in the migrated households has been captured in Table 7. Thanks to government wide campaign, 96-99 per cent of the children are immunised from deadly diseases. However, there are few children left without immunisation. Even, in the case of polio there are children left without immunisation.

Table 7: Child immunisation in the household

Health benefits	*Benefited*	*Not Benefited*	*Not Applicable*
Yashaswini/any other health card	6 (2.20)	266 (97.80)	28
Pregnant women benefit	62 (27.68)	162 (72.32)	76
Girl child benefit (i.e., 1 lakh at the age of 18 years)	05 (29.4)	12	
TB Programme (DOTS)	02 (33.33)	04 (66.66)	294
Special nutrition programme (Vitamin A for < 5 yrs)	45 (26.31)	126 (73.69)	129

Source: Author calculation from household survey.

What emerges from the above analysis is that, many welfare/ security measures failed to identify beneficiaries. Majority of the beneficiaries are not aware of the various education and health schemes meant for them. There is also evidence of procedural delay by the officials in sanctioning the schemes. Though, some of the households have benefited from the schemes, the role of the NGO and political activists in creating awareness about such schemes is nil. Whatever benefits are received by some poor households', majority of them are received through private people i.e., through friends, neighbours, relatives, social and anganwadi workers, health workers. It is very important to bring such groups under safety nets. Suggestions for proper implementation of such programmes and how to bring such groups under safety nets is made in the next section.

IV Conclusion and Suggestions

Health and education play an crucial role in the earning capacity of an individual. For complete improvement of such underprivileged households' and to bring such households to mainstream economic development, providing equitable and affordable health and educational facilities are very important policy options. In the case of education, though the state and central government initiated numbers of schemes to make education affordable to everyone, still large population is illiterate and many children are out of school. Though, with all painful efforts, some underprivileged children are able to study up to X or XII class, but, majority of such children are not able to posses the required skill to get a regular job in the open market. In terms of learning ability and acquisition of skills with having similar degree or class, there is huge difference between underprivileged children and children of affluent families. There is huge difference in quality education imparted in private and government schools. Interestingly, the salary of the teachers of government schools' is substantially higher than that of teachers of private schools. This shows weak monitoring by the government. Majority of underprivileged households are under the illusion that, even with the degree or whatever required educational qualifications, their children can not compete with the children of affluent families in the job market. They are under the impression that providing education for their children beyond the class X is waste. They are interested in providing education to their children up to certain age, the moment children reach certain age and become fit to work in the labour market, poor households start sending their children into workforce. This is one of the important areas, where large reforms are required in this country. Government evaluates its performance in terms of expenditure made on education, enrollment ratio, and expansion of physical infrastructure compared to previous period. There is need to assess in terms of outcome. We need to look at very seriously, whether a child has gained expected aptitude/skill after reaching particular standard or class. Recognising this, the Karnataka state government introduced innovative schemes. The outcome seems only on the paper.

From the interaction with the teachers, concerned government officials, civil society groups and NGO, the identified problems are — (i) lack of commitment by the teachers, (ii) teachers are burdened with so many other government works like census, election duties etc (iii) student teacher ratio is very high, in some cases, more than 100 students per class, per teacher, and one teacher for many classes. In this regard the reforms in education sector with reference to the underprivileged poor households may include; (i) Public – Private partnership: A public-private partnership has the potential of optimising existing resources, as the public sector plays the role of enabler and facilitator, and the private sector contributes its expertise, technology and management practices. (ii) Need to make compulsory for the Private schools to admit the underprivileged children in their school. For such underprivileged children, government has to reimburse the respective school fees. The Delhi government has implemented such scheme, (iii) Need to assess the performance in terms of outcome of the scheme, (iv) Local governments have to be empowered in implementing the schemes, (v) Teacher – student ratio must be ideal, (vi) Teachers should not be over burdened with other government works, (v) Need to establish more number of job oriented training institutions for the underprivileged students after attaining S.S.L.C. Such training institutions should reach all the children of the underprivileged households and (vi) Ultimately, we need to have such an educational policy that after certain level of education, each one should stand on his own. Then only the underprivileged poor households will understand the importance of education for their children.

Health reforms with reference to the underprivileged poor households in India should focus on; (i) Strengthening the Urban Local Bodies (ULB) in designing, implementing, monitoring and evaluating the health schemes for the urban poor households, (ii) Wide campaign on preventive and curative healthcare awareness for such households involving health workers, civil society groups, NGO and students should be undertaken. Government can make compulsory for medical students to visit the slums and survey the health status of all the underprivileged urban households. From such wide survey, people suffering from chronic diseases can be identified. And, can be brought for the treatment, (iii) Like Yeshasvini Health Insurance scheme for rural farmers and peasants in Karnataka, there is need of such schemes for urban slum dwellers also.

References

Gadag District at a Glance (2008-09), Gadag District Administration, Gadag.

Guhan, S (1994): "Social Security Options for Developing Countries", International Labour Review, Vol. 133, No. 1.

Kapoor et al (2008): "The case for Direct Cash Transfer for the Poor" *Economic and Political Weekly,* April 12, 2010.

Planning Commission, First Five Year Plan Document, Government of India. New Delhi.

Planning Commission. 2002. Tenth Five Year Plan. Government of India. New Delhi.

Planning Commission. 2007. Eleventh Five Year Plan. Government of India. New Delhi.

Urban Development Policy of Karnataka (2009), viewed on August 11, 2010. Available at http://www.kuidfc.com/website/webpage.nsf/15a7d0221a9f927265256e7f003a66f6/b3c59be2f8be88265257671003855a9/$FILE/Urban%20Development%20Policy.pdf

Singh, S.P and Agarwal, R.K (1998): "Rural-Urban Migration: The Role of Push and Pull Factors Revisited" The Indian Journal of Labour Economics, Vol. 41, No. 4.

6

Status of Rural Dalit Women in India: A Case Study of Koge Village in Kolhapur District

— P. B. Desai

Introduction

According to the 2011 census there are 16.60 per cent of population belongs scheduled castes and within that nearly half of them are Dalit women. Dalit women are discriminated on three grounds: First they are women they are poor and they Dalits. The urban Dalit women are better off than rural Dalit women. And they are aware of the various government welfare schemes. In case of Dalit women majority of them are illiterate and poor. They hardly had the knowledge of government schemes. According to the NSSO 2009-10 data, 21.90 per cent of Dalit women lives in villages while 14.53 per cent reside in urban areas. Majority of the Dalit women are lives in rural areas and their social, economic and political status is quite different from urban Dalit women. Rural Dalit women are suffer with problems of economic inequality, sexual harassment, lack of economic independence, and lack of credit facilities, and in-access health facilities and also kept them away from decision-making positions which prevent women to participate in formal and informal social organisations.

Dalit women are not only discriminated by people of higher castes, but also within their own communities. Men in Dalit community are always dominant the Dalit women. Dalit women also have less power within the Dalit movement itself. Women are active in large number in movements but most of the leadership positions in the organisations/ associations and local bodies are held by men. So the present paper highlights certain issues and concerns with status of Dalit women in rural areas.

Objectives of the Study

(a) To study Dalit women status in rural areas.

(b) To examine the socio- economic and political status of Dalit women.

Study Area

We have taken Koge village which has 5,500 population from Kolhapur district in Maharashtra for this study. Out of it 800 people belongs to SC community from Mahar, Mang and Chambar Caste.

There are 125 SC households in this village . The main occupation of the villagers is agriculture and they also involved in rearing animal husbandry as an allied occupation. Sugarcane is major crop of the village. The village has Gram Panchayat, co-operative society and Sub-Primary Health Centre. This village is rich and prosperous village.

Methodology

Case study method was used for this research and we have taken four case studies. Informal discussion was held with Dalit women at Koge village of Kolhapur.

Source of Data

The present study was based on the primary as well as secondary data. Primary data was collected through field work and secondary data also obtained from unpublished and published literature concerned with the topic.

Data Analysis and Interpretation

Four case studies were taken from rural Dalit women for this purpose. Their socio-economic background, family and children, their social, economic, and political status and also opinions were ascertained on status of Dalit women and violence against Dalit women in Maharashtra.

Case Study I

Name:- Smt Kalpana Kumar Jadav.

Address:- A/p: Koge, Tal: Karveer, Dist: Kolhapur.

Socio-economic Background

She is 30 years of old and married. She has completed her formal education upto 9th Class. She is working in her own land and also agricultural labourer in others land. She is member of Self-Help-Group.

About her Family and children

She is having nuclear family with four members and she has one son and one daughter. Her family has 10 guntas of cultivable land and agriculture is the main source of income. She also rear animal husbandry. Her annual income from all source is Rs/30,000 only. When we asked about girl education. She agreed that girl should be given education,by which she can be economically independent. She also agreed there is no open caste discrimination in the school.

Social, economical and political Status

The caste discrimination is there but in an invisible way. She also participate actively in the public functions of the village. She is not aware about the schemes for SC. She also told that there is no any type of violence against women in village and poverty is major problem of rural Dalit women.

Opinion about Dalit women and violence against Dalit women in Maharashtra

The status of Dalit women is improving. Dalit women do participate in the village politics and contest village elections. Violence against Dalit women in Maharashtra is also increasing.

Case Study II

Name: Miss. Nikita Suresh Khabade

Address: - A/p: Koge, Tal: Karveer, Dist: Kolhapur.

Socio-economic Background

She is 19 years unmarried Dalit women. She studied upto 8th Class. She also work as agricultural labourer in the village. As she is not married and also due to family restriction she didn't join any groups in the village.

About her Family and children

Being un-married member of five members family does not hold any responsibility as well as share in the family. Her family works as a agricultural labourers in village. Besides that she also do the tailoring job in the evenings.Her annual income from all the sources is Rs/35,000. She was asked about the welfare scheme implemented in the village she said no knowledge.

Social, economical and political Status

There is caste discrimination openly but an invisible way of discrimination were been noticed by her in the village. She is not aware about the schemes for SC. She also told that there is no any type of violence against women in village.

Case Study III

Name: Kajal Amoll Kamble

Address: - A/p: Koge, Tal: Karveer, Dist: Kolhapur.

Socio-economic Background

She is 22 years of old and married. She has completed her formal education upto 11th Std. She works in her own land and also agricultural labourer in other's land. She is member of Self-Help-Group.

About her Family and children

She is having family with three members and she has 10 gunt land

land. She is a agricultural labourer. Her annual income from all sources Rs/20,000 rupees.

Opinion about status of Dalit women and violence against Dalit women in Maharashtra

Overall status of Dalit women is changing. Dalit women are taking active part in the village politics. Violence against Dalit women in Maharashtra is increasing. Even though in some villages of Maharashtra there is caste discrimination.

Case Study IV

Name: Smt Manisha Rohit Sathpute.

Address: A/p: Koge, Tal: Karveer, Dist:

Kolhapur.

Socio-economic Background: She is 23 years of old and married. She has completed teacher training course. She is working as teaching assistant.

About her Family and children: She is newly Married women living with nuclear family with no cultivable land. She is a employed women. Her annual income is 20, 000.When question was asked about girl education, she agreed that overall development of individual is dependent on education. So girl should be educated.

Social, economical and political Status: There is caste discrimination openly but an invisible way of discrimination were been noticed by her in the village. She never face any type of violence at home. She is aware about the schemes for SC. She also told that there is no any type of violence against women in village. Here she mentioned poverty, high prices of goods, not overall improvement of community and lack of professional and higher education among Dalit women are major problem of rural Dalit women in village.

Opinion about Dalit women and violence against Dalit women in Maharashtra: Dalit women are taking active participation in politics and public functions. They are member of gram panchayat, taluka panchayat and zilla panchayat. But their decision is not taken into consideration and there is no value for their decision.

Major Findings

- Majority of Dalit women in the study area are working as agriculture labourers and the average age of these women are between 19 to32.
- Their Income is meager. Their annual income from all sources is between Rs/ 20,000 to Rs/50,000 rupees.
- Poverty is major problem of rural Dalit women.
- Based on the above study there is no violence against women in village, but they told that violence against Dalit women in other villages of Maharashtra is increasing.
- Personally they did not face any caste discrimination in schools, public places and at work place. But still there is caste discrimination at some level.
- Most of women are actively participating in the public affairs.
- They told that their children those who are studying in the school are not facing any caste discrimination.
- All women believe girls' education and they are eager allow the girls' to get education.
- Dalit women are taking active participation in politics and public functions.
- They are member of gram panchayat, taluka panchayat and zilla panchayat. But their decision is not taken into consideration and there is no value for their decision.
- Very few are getting higher education. But number is not higher than the urban Dalit women.
- Dalit Women are not aware about government welfare schemes for SC. But they told that young educated people are well aware about these schemes.
- These women are not much aware about how caste discrimination is manipulated in the village. Still there is caste discrimination in the village but its manifestations are different.
- When informal discussion was held with rural dalit women of Koge Village in Kolhapur district they expressed that their main problem is poverty is the major problem of them.

Improvement of community and education of rural Dalits are very essential.

Conclusion

Majority of rural Dalit women are either illiterate or studied upto primary and secondary level. New Economic Policy has seriously impacted their livelihoods particularly the mechnisation of agriculture. On the other hand, irregular monsoons also created havoc in the poor and agriculturally dependent families because they don't have alternative source of income. Due to this there is an urgency to increase the non-agricultural sector where the rural Dalit women can earn their livelihoods.

References

J. Muthumary, Professor, Centre for Advanced Studies in Botony, University of Madras, Guindy Campus, Chennai 600 working paper on "Dalit Women in India".

Gopal Guru, (1995), "Dalit Women Talk Differently", *Economic and Political Weekly,* Vol. 30, No. 41/42 (Oct. 14-21, 1995), pp. 2548-2550.

P. Ashalatha (2013),"Status of Dalit Women in India- Caste and Gender Based Exclusion" Paripex - *Indian Journal of Research*, Volume : 2 | Issue : 2 | February 2013 ISSN - 2250-1991.

Paik, Shailaja, (2009), "Amchya Jalmachi Chittarkatha (The Bioscope of Our Lives): Who Is My Ally?, *Economic and Political Weekly,* Vol. 44, No. 40 (OCTOBER 3-9, 2009), pp. 39-47.

Sharma, Nandita,(2012), "The status of Dalit Women in India- from Deprivity to Supremacy", Lapis Lazuli –An International Literary Journal / Vol.II/ Issue I /SPRING 2012 ISSN 2249-4529.

Srivastava, Sumit S. (2007), "Violence and Dalit Women's Resistance in Rural Bihar" in *Journal of Indian Anthropologist*, Vol. 37, No. 2 (July-Dec. 2007), pp. 31-44, published by: Indian Anthropological Association.

htpp//www.pintersociety.com

http://www.ambedkar.org/Worldwide_Dalits/dalit_women_in_India.htm

http://dalitvision.blogspot.in/2015/03/socio-economic-status-of-dalit-women.html

http://www.indianet.nl/pdf/StatusDalitWomen.pdf

http://www.ohchr.org/Documents/HRBodies/CEDAW/RuralWomen/FEDONavsarjanTrustIDS.pdf

http://www.publicpolicy.in/status-of-dalit-women-gaps-in-educational-attainment-and- economic-opportunities/

7

Access to Land and Livelihoods of Rural Dalits in Dakshina Kannada District, Karnataka

— *G. Srikantha Nayaka, Ramakrishnappa, V and ProfessorVishwanatha*

Introduction

In most parts of India, there is a correlation between economic status and the structural position of castes. The reason is that, historically, higher castes had better access to occupations, income and assets than lower castes. In Hindu society, occupation was one of the defining features of the caste hierarchy, with socially valued occupations bestowing high socio-economic status on caste members. In the modern context, there has been a loosening of the caste – occupation linkage. A dynamic occupational shift has not occurred however and high-end jobs continue to be the preserve of the 'upper' castes and, now, increasingly, high-income classes. Government policies have ensured that there has been a significant degree of occupational diversity among the SCs but a large percentage of the SC population, especially the exuntouchable castes among the Scheduled Castes, still constitutes a sizable chunk of the low income population with poor human development indicators. In Karnataka, as in other parts of the country, the Scheduled Castes are largely concentrated in the rural parts of the state. Almost 75 per cent SCs live in villages and depend upon agricultural labour or agriculture-related activities for subsistence.

Those who have migrated to cities have taken up occupations such as construction work, street sweeping and other manual labour, which again are not very remunerative. Only a few are engaged in trade and commerce. The reservation policy has ensured that many SCs entered government service and reached to higher echelons of the power structure, but they comprise only a fraction of their population in the state. The majority languishes in low-end jobs, on the fringe of the poverty line.

Objectives of the Study: The purpose of the present study is

1. To understand the occupational pattern among rural dalits.
2. To analyse the land ownership pattern among rural dalits.
3. To assess the trends in operational holdings across social groups and study the problems being faced by the *dalit* households in access to land.

Economic Status of Dalits in India

Majority of the Schedule Caste population lives in rural areas, which is characterised as an agrarian economy. The poverty ratio, the size of the land holding, occupational classification and number of main workers and its pattern are important parameters to judge the rural economy. Most of the SC families are still below poverty line. Majority of them are engaged in low wage and even obnoxious and degraded occupations like sweeping and scavenging. Their skill base is rather weak. The major occupational groups of SCs can be categorised into

1. Agricultural labourers – (a) landless, (b) those with petty extent of agricultural land.
2. Marginal and small cultivators including share croppers and other tenants.
3. Fishermen.
4. Traditional Artisans – (a) Leather workers, (b) Weavers, (c) Other artisans.

5. Civic Sanitation workers (scavengers and sweepers), and Traditional Dais.
6. Urban marginal labour.
7. The educated.

These occupational groups may be put into two broad categories, namely

1. Those engaged in land-based activities.
2. Those engaged in non-land based activities.

In In dia, the Hindu society is divided into various castes on the basis of their occupation. In the lowest rank of this classification are the Scheduled Castes (SCs) who are condemned to perform the menial and unclean tasks on behalf of the society. As they were exclusively assigned the role of performing unclean tasks on behalf of the society, they came to be treated as outcastes or "untouchables". It is this social stigma that pushed them down to the bottom of the social ladder alienating them from the mainstream of the society and assigning them to a position lower than several depressed classes who also suffered from social, economic and educational deprivation. A look at the recent available data brings out these facts quite clearly. About three-fourths of the SCs live in rural areas, where the main source of livelihood is either farming, wage labour or some kind of non-farm business. In 2000, only 16 per cent of all SC households cultivated land as owner-cultivator as against 41 per cent among non-SC/ST households. Only 12 per cent carryout some kind of business, which indicates access to capital. Taking both farm and non-farm activities, only about 28 per cent of rural households had got some access to capital assets as compared to 56 per cent for non-SC/ST households.

Access to land in an agriculture-based rural economy is important because land is a primary means and instrument of production. The social distribution of land in a village economy determines the economic position and power relations between different social groups in the village. The share of dalits (SC households) in terms of land ownership has not been rising in proportion to their share in the population. In rural areas the main source of livelihood of SCs is either farming, wage labour or some kind of non-farm business. In 2000, only 16 per cent of all SC households cultivated land as owner as against 41 per cent among non-SC/ST households. Taking both farm and non-farm activities, only about 28 per cent of rural households have got access to capital assets as compared to 56 per cent of non-SC/ST households (Planning Commission, 2008). The dalits are predominantly agricultural labourers and most of them are landless.

Land ownership patterns in Karnataka

Scheduled Caste ownership of agricultural land is minimal and the majority of landholders have small and unviable holdings. Progressive policies such as the Karnataka Land Reforms Act 1961 and various administrative measures of the government under this Act and Rules, have made it possible for many SC tenant cultivators to become land owners. Under the land distribution scheme, out of the surplus land identified by the government, only 18,361 SC agricultural labourers and marginal landholders were allotted about 69,893 acres of agricultural land in the 1990s.

According to the Humann Development report 2005 reveals that out of a total 70.79 lakh operational holdings, 8.23 lakh (11.65 per cent) are owned by SCs. The total area cultivated by SCs is 10.71 lakh hectare out of a total operated area of 123.07 lakh hectare, accounting for 8.7 per cent. Since SCs comprise 16.21 per cent of the total population of the state, it is clear that their ownership of agricultural land holdings is not commensurate with their share of the population.

As shown in the Table-1 that 52 per cent of marginal (less than one hectare) and 30 per cent of small (1–2 hectare) operational holdings were held by SCs while non-SCs held about 45 per cent and 26 per cent of marginal and small holdings respectively. It is evident that the share of operational holdings decreases as the size of holdings increases for SCs as well as for all groups. An important feature is that the marginal and small operational holdings of the SCs which form about 82 per cent of total SC holdings account for a little more than half (53 per cent) of the total operated area belonging to SCs. As against this, 72 per cent of the marginal and small holdings of non-SCs and non-STs, account for about 32.4 per cent of the total operated area.

Table 1: Distribution of operational holdings and operated areas by major size class for different social groups in Karnataka: 2001

Size	*Scheduled Castes*		*Scheduled Tribes*		*Others*		*Total*	
	Number of Holdings	*Area*	*Number of Holdings*	*Area*	*Number of Holdings*	*Area*	*Number of Holdings*	*Area*
Marginal	52.13	19.70	40.84	12.00	45.41	11.40	45.94	12.20
Small	30.13	33.10	30.89	25.30	26.28	21.10	26.98	22.40
Semi - medium	13.73	27.70	19.37	29.60	18.26	27.90	17.79	28.00
Medium	3.65	16.00	7.85	25.30	8.65	28.30	8.03	27.00
Large	0.36	3.50	1.05	7.70	1.40	11.40	1.26	10.50
	100	100	100	100	100	100	100	100

Sources: Karnataka Human Development Report (2005).

The majority of SC cultivators own marginal and small holdings, which are not viable and drive them towards indebtedness and poverty. It could be argued that, for majority of SC cultivators owning agricultural land has become a symbol of security rather than a major source of income.

A Demographic Features of Scheduled Castes, Dakshina Kannada District in Karnataka

The 'Scheduled Castes' refer to castes, races or groups within such castes, races or tribes as are deemed under Article 341 of the Constitution of India. The Constitution of India authorises the President of India to specify such castes or tribes to be notified as SCs and STs. The Scheduled Castes people in Dakshina Kannada district, belonging to Ajila, Bakuda, Bhaira, Godda, Holeya, Mogera, Mundala, Nalkedaya, Parava, Pambada, Raneyar and Samagara. They are traditionally involved in such pursuits like scavenging, leather work and agricultural labourers.

Amongst these communities, Nalkedaya, Parava, Pambada and Raneyar are supposed to be the most backward. They live in the villages with others. Nalkedaya, Parava and Pambada communities are the main communities who participate in Bhoota Kola (act as possessed one in spiritual tradition). Generally, Nalkedaya population do not own lands, whereas, some Paravas are landowners. They are mainly involved in their traditional family pursuits (Bhoota Kola) during 4-5 months in a year. Rest of the time, they earn their livelihood through labour. Amongst Raneyar community, majority are labourers and work mainly as masons and construction workers. This community is relatively in small number. In individually SCs, there are sub-castes having distinctly different traditions and culture and hereditary pursuits.

According to the 2011 census, the district has 1,48,178 SC populations (Table 2). They constitute 7.09 per cent of the total district population. The district has one of the lowest per cent of the SC and among 30 districts in the state. Taluk-wise, Mangaluru taluk has the highest percentage of the SC population (33 per cent), followed by Puttur (23 per cent) and Belthangady (17 per cent). Bantwal has the lowest SC population of 13 per cent. Sullia has slightly higher SC population (13.7 per cent). As regards STs, Bantwal has the highest population (25 per cent), followed by Puttur (21 per cent) and Mangaluru (20 per cent). Belthangady has 19 per cent and Sulla has the lowest, 14 per cent. The majority of SCs live in rural areas. Nearly 69 per cent of the SCs are in rural areas and remaining 31 per cent of the SCs are residing in urban areas.

Table 2: Population of Scheduled Castes in Dakshina Kannda (As per 2011 Census)

Taluk	*2011 Census Numbers*		
	Male	*Female*	*Total*
Bantawal	9585	9675	19260
Belthangadi	12426	12890	25316
Mangalore	24262	25013	49275
Puttur	17102	16938	34040
Sullia	9949	10338	20287
District	**73324**	**74854**	**148178**

Sources: Dakshina Kannada District - Human Development Report - 2014.

Status of Landless Households in Dakshina Kannada

The land is the main income generating asset in rural areas. Poverty is also closely related to ownership of assets. For the landless people, the labour is only their asset and wage employment is the only source of survival. In rural areas, the landless households usually belong to landless agricultural labourers and include SCs and STs. No reliable data is, however, available on landless households. The agricultural labourers in the district, as per 2011 census, are 24,854. All agricultural labourers cannot be treated as landless. The land holding distribution pattern in different taluks in the district is analysed in detail in the above paragraphs. The marginal farmers cultivating below 1 hectare constitute 73 per cent of farming community. The average size of land holding of marginal farmers is 0.38 hectare. With the present mono cropping pattern and cropping intensity, these farmers would not be in a position to earn a net income of even US $1.25 per day, which is the World Bank's indicator of poverty line for classifying the poorest of the poor in the world. Since the marginal farmers in the district have to depend on labour for their livelihood, they can be considered as constituent belonging to landless households.

Table 3 shows that the taluk-wise data on the landless households. At the outset, it should be noted that there is a possibility of one family owning more than one agricultural land holding and to that extent, the estimates of landless households are underestimated. The total number of landless households in the district as per this estimate is 16,146, which works out to 7 per cent of the total rural households. Taluk-wise Belthangady and Mangaluru taluks have the highest number of landless households. Puttur has the lowest number of landless households. Sullia has 2,195 households without land. It is also important to note that among 20,416 SC households in rural areas, SC cultivators are 10,959. Nearly 9,457 SC households are landless. Their percentage works out to 46.3 per cent. In the case of STs, out of 13,111 households, 9,618 households are cultivators and 3,493 are landless. The percentage of ST landless households works out to 26.6 per cent. The landless households in STs mainly belong to Koraga community who are the poorest of the poor in Dakshina Kannada district.

Table 3: Landless Households in Dakshina Kannada District

Taluk	*Total Rural Households*	*No. of Agricultural land holders (Number)*	*Landless Households*
Bantawal	54562	54008	554
Belthangadi	52151	43375	8776
Mangalore	44003	39645	4358
Puttur	46647	46384	263
Sullia	27880	25685	2195
District	**225243**	**209097**	**16145**

Sources: Dakshina Kannada District - Human Development Report - 2014.

Occupational Pattern and Livelihood Opportunities

The livelihood status of SCs and STs depends on their access to productive assets and resources as well as the employment pattern. Traditionally, the SCs were landless bonded agricultural labourers.

Their principal asset was their labour. The STs were mainly a tribal community engaged in subsistence farming in forest areas, hunting and gathering forest products and basket making. Nearly 76 per cent of the SC families and 85 per cent of ST families live in rural areas. At present, in rural areas, nearly 48 per cent of the SC families are landless agricultural labourers. Out of 20,416 SC rural families, 10,539 (52 per cent) are having agricultural landholdings. In urban areas, they are mostly involved in sanitation and cleaning and construction works. Among 11,087 ST families living in rural areas, 9,618 (87 per cent) have agricultural land (Table 4).

Table 4: Agricultural Land Holding Pattern of SCs and STs in Dakshina Kannada District

Size of Land Holdings	*Scheduled Castes*			*Scheduled Tribes*		
	Number	*Area*	*Average Size*	*Number*	*Area*	*Average Size*
Below	9224	3483.23	0.38	7455.77	3155.77	0.42
1-2	1171	1569.95	1.34	1825	2474.72	1.36
2-4	140	337.46	2.41	336	828.41	2.46
4-10	4	18.44	4.61	26	126.36	2.46
10 and above						
Total	**10539**	**5409.085**	**0.51**	**9618**	**6585.26**	**0.68**

Source: Dakshina Kannada District at a Glance, 2011-12.

As regards landholding pattern among SCs and STs, 87.5 per cent of the SC farmers are marginal farmers with average size of landholding of 0.38 ha. Marginal farmers and small farmers having 1 to 2 hactares together constitute 98.6 per cent of total SC farmers. Only 144 SC families have landholding above 2 ha. In the case of ST farmers, 77 per cent are marginal farmers with average size of land holding of 0.42 ha. Marginal farmers and small farmers having 1 to 2 ha, together constitute 96 per cent of total ST farming community. Out of 9,618 ST farmers, only 362 have landholding above 2 ha. From this it is evident that almost all SC and ST farmers for their livelihood have to depend on agricultural labour. With the present non-viability of monocropping pattern and the slow-down in the agriculture, the SCs and STs farmers in rural areas are increasingly becoming marginalised and entering into labour market for their livelihood. In rural areas, out of 20,416 SC families, 9,877 (48 per cent) are the landless households.

References

Govt of Karnataka (2005). Human Development Report 2015, Bengaluru.

Dakshina Kannada District at a Glance (2011-12), Mangalore.

Govt of Karnataka Dakshina Kannada District - Human Development Report – 2014.

Govt of India (2006). Scheduled Caste Sub Plan Planning Commission, New Delhi.

Planning Commission (2012-17). 'Twelfth Five Year Plan (2012–2017), Social Sectors, Vol. III, Government of India, New Delhi.

8

Democratic Decentralisation and Nature of Political Exclusion of Dalits in Panchayati Raj

— Avinash G Bhale

Introduction

The history of local self governances and its significant feature of the governance is to empower the people at grassroot level. With this objective only the Constitutional Amendment Act has be passed by the Parliament. The 73rd and 74th Amendments to the Constitution of India are also popularly known as the 'Panchayati Raj Act', in which legal status has been sanctioned to rural and urban governments which was not there in the earlier case. Indian government is the largest representative and democratic governance in the world. Different thinkers and practitioners argue that "Democratic Decentralisation" would be a greatest force for good governance in terms of inclusion and securing the participation of excluded groups at all levels of governance.

At the larger picture particularly in International level, majority of the developing countries in the world today have adopted decentralised form of administration, especially after 1980s. Decentralisation is a developmental strategy that has emerged as a dominant trend in the world politics. Decentralisation has been looked as a useful mode of governance to deliver the goods to public at suitable and convenient way. To bring the administration at the doorsteps of the citizens and also to establish a direct relationship between the people and administration is best form governance in the developing countries. All the United Notions agencies, international financial institutions, and national and local governments are promoting and supporting decentralisation on the argument that, lower tiers of the administration can better serve the people in the developmental efforts with more effectively and efficiently than the central and state governments.

In a globalised era, it would be difficult to see the actual problem at grassroot level. Different national, international actors and stakeholders play different roles in the political and economic domain of the country, especially country like India where there is market potentiality to all these actors in such situations the local people get affected by their projects in that situations local self governances can play dominant role to deliver the services while implementing the rehabilitation package more effective manner to these specific targeted people.

The process of land acquisition and setting up projects along with rehabilitation to displaced or affected people is a major concern of the current state of development. Panchayati Raj institution can play a meaningful role in this whole development process at local level. The decision-making process at local level are necessary for such development issues. In the presence of feudal set up implementation of such schemes would be a challenging task.

Decentralisation and community driven management acquire special importance in the context of the ongoing process of globalisation. While the process of globalisation acts in ways in which circumstances the market acquires supremacy over the people who lost control over their livelihood patterns and this could be ascertained through the process of decentralisation as a countervailing force to enable them to acquire in decision making in their favour.

Research methodology

Both **quantitative and qualitative research design** is used for the current study; **Survey Method** is used for the current study. There are 131 villages in Panhala Block out of 16 villages took randomly for data. We divide the small town into two clusters. One side of the Panhala fort cluster covers Awali, Bongewadi, Jakhale, Kakhe, Kodoli, Mitharwadi, Mohair, Vekhandwadi. The second cluster which covers the villages down from Panhala fort which has Alave, Ghotavade, Majanal, Nevada, Padal, Patpanhala, Pimple T. Thane, Yevluj villages. 482 respondents were selected, with the help simple stratified random sampling method. Information regarding the profile of the villages and the list of the respondents were gathered through government sources by visiting the Phanala Panchayat Samiti office. The rest of the information was collected from respondent's. Responses and views related Gram panchayat and nature of their participation in Gram panchayat activity in the light of 73rd Amendment was gathered through structured interviews. Since the study is based on interview method. The interview schedules were canvassed for final field study in a Phanala block of Kolhapur. Besides this; the observation method was also used to collect data on certain issues like rural political leadership. This method was applied to substantiate with original date or with interview data. The observation method was used in three broad contexts; (i) while interviewing respondents, (ii) while visiting Panchayat offices, and (iii) while visiting villages during the field work. The information gathered from observation is used as additional information to the study and to understand the issues which are need to deal with more holistic and comprehensive way.

Objectives of the study

1. To study the participation of marginalised communities role in the 73rd Constitutional Amendment.
2. To asses the decision-making process in the Panchayat meetings.
3. To draw a conclusion about the level of participation of marginalised communities in Panchayati Raj institutions and to identify the obstructing factors for effective participation.
4. To understand the gender and caste dynamics and their impact on their participation at these institutions.

73rd Amendment in India

The Constitution (73rd Amendment) Act, 1992 mandates provisions for:–

1. Establishment of a three-tier structure of Panchayats.
2. To provide a 3-tier system of Panchayati Raj for all States having a population of over 20 lakh.
3. Establishment of Gram Sabhas at the village level.
4. Regular elections to Panchayats every 5 years.
5. Proportionately reservation of seats to the Scheduled Castes and Scheduled Tribes.
6. Reservation of not less than 33 per cent seats for women.
7. Constitution of State Finance Commissions to make recommendations regarding the financial powers of the Panchayats.
8. Constitution of District Planning Committee to prepare draft development plan for the district as a whole.

Powers and Responsibilities: The Constitution (73rd Amendment) Act, 1992 vests power in the State Government to endow Panchayats with such powers and authority as may be necessary to enable them to function as institutions of selfgovernment such as: -

1. Preparation of plants and their execution for economic development and social justice in relation to 29 subjects listed in the XI Schedule of the Constitution.
2. Authority to levy, collect and appropriate taxes, duties, tolls and fees to Panchayats.
3. Transfer of taxes, duties, tolls and fees collected by the States to Panchayats.

Gram Sabha

In the Panchayati Raj set up, the Gram Sabha, the general assembly of villagers has a key role in the effective functioning of Panchayats. In the Gram Sabha meeting, the rural poor, the women, and the marginalised people would get an opportunity to get involved in decisions making process. Active participation in the Gram Sabha would ensure a participatory democracy with transparency, accountability.

1. Gram Sabha should meet at least once a quarter preferably on Republic Day, Labour Day, Independence Day and Gandhi Jayanti.
2. Decide developmental work to be undertaken by Panchayats based on the needs assessment.
3. Suggest remedial measures for economy and efficiency in the functioning of the Panchayats.
4. Question and scrutinizing the decisions of Panchayats in the meeting of Gram Sabha.
5. Discuss the Annual Financial Statement of Gram Panchayats.

The Constitution (73rd Amendment) Act, 1992 envisages empowered the Panchayats as institutions of self-government at the village level:

1. Planning and executing the village level public works and their maintenance.
2. The ensuring the welfare of the people at the village level including health, education, communal harmony, social justice particularly gender and caste-based discrimination, dispute resolution, the welfare of children, especially the girl-child.

The Constitution (73rd Amendment) Act, 1992 also envisages to empowered Gram Sabhas as the Parliament of the People at the grassroots level to whom the Gram Panchayats are solely accountable.

Political Exclusion of Dalits

Influences in the election process and politics in the village

In Indian, the power structure in the society is dominated by the upper castes. Despite their prominence by a few Dalits in high political positions they are allowed to exercise the powers sanctioned to them by Constitutionally. The current study try to tap the existing practices at village level in Kolhapur. It has been observed in this study that in all the villages upper caste male are dominating all the political activities like nominating, and electing representatives in the village level. As per our observation in the study, we found that all the elections at village level are run by the upper caste and economically powerful class of the village and they always get affiliated to either regional or national political party. This strategy has been working very effectively at Gram panchayat level but if one looks into the realities it all together show different picture from the excluded groups perspective. As it can observe from the following Table 1.

Table 1: Caste and Influences on the election process and politics in Village

Caste	*Influences on the election process and politics in village*						
	Landlord	*Upper caste people*	*Peoples with political relation*	*Majority panel*	*Individual-centric*	*3 and 2*	*Total*
Open	0.4	0.6	11.8	18.9	1.7	8.5	41.9
OBC	0.8	1.7	11.4	6.4	1.2	7.3	28.8
SC and ST	0.4	0.4	2.7	4.6	1	13.5	22.6
NTDNT	0	0	0.4	2.9	0.4	2.9	6.6
Total	**1.6**	**2.7**	**26.3**	**32.8**	**4.3**	**32.2**	**100**

Source: Field Data.

13.5 per cent of the respondents from SC and ST says upper caste people from the majority panel has greater influences on the political process at the village level, 8.5 per cent respondent belong from dominated caste also respond in the same way. Form the table 32.8 per cent respondent saying majority panel influences on the political process. Only 26.3 percent respondent says the people with political affiliation as influences on the all political process at the village level. Due to this, elections in the villages are not always free and fair.

Because of affiliation, upper catse, Maratha community play a dominant role in management of power structure at the village level.

Caste and Respondents' participation or attendance in the Gram sabha

Decentralisation is no doubt a multi-dimensional concept. Gram Sabha is an institutional mechanism of participatory democracy. It provides an opportunity to all the people to participate in the developmental process. 'Gram Sabha' means a body consisting of all the voters in the village. This has been considered as a model democracy at the grassroots where direct participation by the people.

Table 2: Caste and Respondent's participation or attendances in Gramsabha Cross tabulation

Caste	*Respondent's participation or attendances in Gramsabha*		
	No	*Yes*	*Total*
Open	13.5	28.4	41.9
OBC	11.2	17.6	28.8
SC and ST	14.3	8.3	22.6
NTDNT	2.5	4.1	6.6
Total	**41.5**	**58.4**	**100**

Source: Field Data.

Gram sabha is one of the important tool for democracy which secures participation of the people in the democratic process. During the study, we asked the questions about the respondents participation in the Gram Sabha. Only 8.3 per cent people out of 22.6 per cent of Dalit respondent attend the Gram sabha and this implies that only the elected members of dalit family are attending the meetings. Remaining 14.3 per cent responded out of 22.6 per cent Dalit respondent's not attending Gram sabha due to various reasons. *It is distinctly seen that Participation of the Dalits communities in the Gram Sabha is very nominal in the study area.* Why the Dalits not able to attending the gram sabha is a very important question in the context of democratic decentralisation.

In the study area, they use different methods or practices to call and conduct a Gram Sabha, unlike the existing procedures. Since the date and time of Gram sabha is so important for successful participation of the villagers in the Gram sabha and they never follow the same procedure to conduct Gram sabha. Due to this, villagers hardly take part in the Gram sabha. With references to chart 3, out of 22.65 percent only 2.1 to 2.7 per cent dalit respondents responded that they receive the information on Gram sabha through the notice and Davandi (which is a local method for conducting the Gram Sabha) and 12.4 percent of dalit respondents are received information from other sources.

The most important thing is no one received information from panchayat office and majority of them received information after Gram Sabha is over. But ironically in the case of Marathas 13.5 per cent out of 41.9 per cent receive information same as the case with OBC out of 28.8 per cent only 7.9 per cent OBC respondent received.

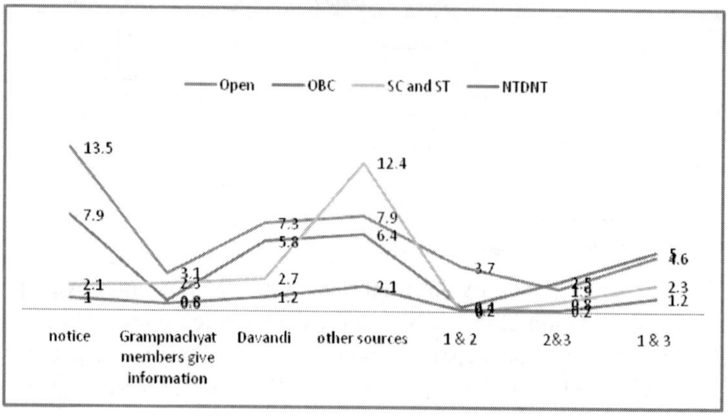

Source: Field Data.

Caste and information sources related Gramsabha

Based on the above inference one can have to a conclusion that both village level staff a well as the upper caste are intentionally keeping the dalit out of the Gram Sabha meetings. They not only keeping them away and also trying their level best not share the political power at local level. This indicates that the 73rd Constitutional Amendment Act has empower the marginalised groups on paper not on reality.

Reasons for Dalit Exclusion from Local Self-Governance

There are different reasons have been reported by the research team for Dalit exclusion from Local self Governance by different caste groups.

Table 3: Caste and caste responses on Dalit exclusion from Local self-Governance

Caste	*Responses on Dalit exclusion from Local self-Governance*					
	They are illiterate hence, they don't understand the importance of it	*Time of Gramsabha and job time is same*	*Political isolation by the other communities*	*No information*	*No response*	*Total*
Open	8.5	17.2	7.3	6	2.9	41.9
OBC	10.4	11.2	3.5	2.7	1	28.8
SC and ST	6.2	9.5	5.2	0.6	1	22.6
NTDNT	1.5	3.9	0.6	0	0.6	6.6
Total	**26.6**	**41.8**	**16.6**	**9.3**	**5.5**	**100**

Source: Field Data.

With references to above the Table 3 that 41.8 percent respondents says that the Gram Sabha meeting is clashing with their daily wage due to this they are unable to participate in the Gram Sabha. They also say Gram Sabha or participation in Gram sabha is not important than their livelihood. With this conclusion, one can draw an attention that majority of the dalits in the study area are landless and agricultural labours and they mainly work in the firms of upper caste landlords only.

In case if they try to assert their political rights at village level and their livelihoods will always at stake. Of the total respondents 26.6 per cent are illiterates respondents and they do not possess any kind political capacities and also they don't understand the importance of Gramsabha.16.6 per cent respondent's from all categories say that the political class in the village always keep them away from local politics.

Due to the avobe reasons Dalits are not capable of participating in the local politics because of their livelihood insecurity,second illiteracy and negative feeling among these groups towards the Gram Sabha, thirdly they are politically isolated by the dominated community and lastly, they are contentiously kept away from panchayat politics.

Participation process of upper caste women and Dalit women in Panchayati Raj

In Accident India (3200 BC), the caste system was nonexistent since even the most learned men were good householders and had varied occupations. The accident women were just as superior as men in learning; education and intellect. But the creation of a number of Hindu religious books, including the Manusmriti, Atharva Vedas Vishnu Smriti and strong institutionalisation of the teachings and sayings in these books create inequality between men and women. B. R. Ambedkar makes it very clear in his Article titled “The rise and fall of Hindu woman” that the root causes of sufferings of women in India are these all books, Manusmriti divided the society in a stratified way and it promoted inequality among men and women and also within the community. According to Manusmriti, women have no right to education, independence or wealth.

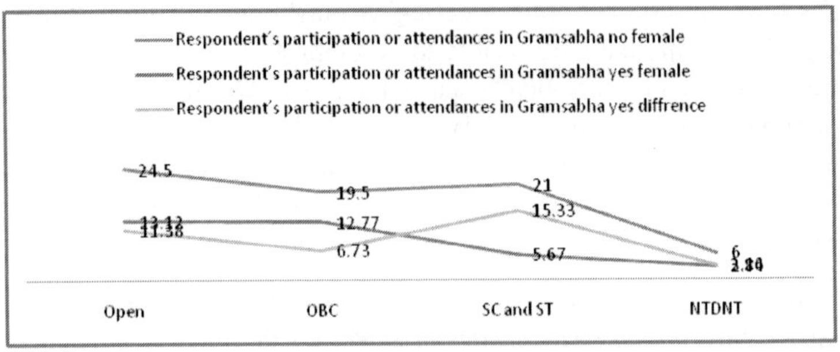

Source: Field data.

Castewise Particpation of Women in Gramsabha

With references to above chart, it is clearly seen that 24.5 per cent upper caste women, never attend Gram sabha and the remaining 13.12 percent attend the gram sabha. In the case of OBC also 19.5 5 never attend Gram sabha only 6.73 per cent OBC Women mainly those are elected members. Within Dalit women 21 per cent Dalit women not attends the gram sabha and only 5.67 per cent Dalit women mainly those are elected members attending gram sabha. If we see the differences we will find Dalit women participation is very low compared to OBC and open upper caste women.

Conclusion

Based on the inference drawn from primary data on the participation of excluded groups in the Panhala block of Kolhapur district suggests that the excluded groups have not taken active role in the Gram sabha. A number factors are have been identified for this and they are: "Not informed regarding Gram sabha" is a strategy keep them away from participating in the political process at local level. Along the above finding we can read that in the study area, mostly excluded communities like Dalits are not capable of participating in the Gram sabha due to major four reasons, firstly, they don't take time due to livelihood insecurity; secondly, illiteracy and negative feeling among these groups towards the Gram panchayat or political process, thirdly, they are politically isolated from the other dominated community and Lastly, they kept didn't inform related to Gram sabha. It is a readable delineation of the participation of upper caste women in the political operation in local self-governances and within 27.01 per cent women respondent from the open community mostly is elected members and therefore, they accept to attend Gramsabha.

At the local level, powers have been decentralised but the livelihood linkages and their dependency on upper caste still play a vital role in the policy inclusion. Total village level political spaces are enjoyed by the upper caste community. So "Decentralisation of powers" to claim ideally looks very good to see at the grassroots level is very difficult to implement due to caste system and its prejudices. Though the 73rd Amendment gives powers but asserting of powers by the Dalit will always lead Atrocities against Dalits across the country.

References

Mani Shankar Iyer: 'The Panchayat System: A Major Innovation in Empowering People" address by the Minister of Panchayati Raj government of India at the conference on 'Making Democratic Governments Work- Connecting Principle and Practice' at the Ash Institute for Democratic Governance and Innovation, Harvard University, April 2005.

Sudha Menon (2007): Grass-root Democracy and Empowerment of People: Evolution of Panchayati Raj in India, MPRA Paper No. 3839, posted 5.

Ruth, J. Alsop (2008): Inclusion and local elected governments: the Panchayat raj system in India, World Bank India.

Singh, Raj: Panchayat Raj Manual: A Socio-Historical Cum Legal Perspective, Anmol Publications, New Delhi, 1996, p. 10.

Ghosh, Rathna, Pramanik, Alok Kumar: Panchayat System in India. Historical, Constitutional and Financial Analysis, Kanishka Publication, New Delhi, 1999, p. 208.

Singh, Raj, Panchayat Raj Manual : A Socio-Historical Cum Legal Perspective, 1996.

Mathew, George: Panchayati Raj in India, An Overview. Status of Panchayati Raj in India, Concept Publishing Company, New Delhi, 2000, p. 3.

Altekar, A.S.: State and Government in Ancient India, Motilal Banarasi Das Publications, New Delhi, 1997, p. 229.

Prabhat Datta (1998): Major Issues in the Development Debate, New Delhi : Kanishka, pp. 14-19.

9

Violation of Dalit Human Rights-A Study in Andhra Pradesh

—Akepogu Jammanna,
Pasala Sudhakar

> *"You are made to suffer wants, privation and humiliations not because it was preordained by the sins committed in your previous birth but because of the overpowering tyranny and treachery of those who are about you. You have no lands because others usurped them; you have no posts because others have monopolised them. Do not believe in* fate. Believe in your strength.*"* **– B.R. Ambedkar**

All human societies are aspire for peace, stability and prosperity in all times. The holy texts of all religions speak about human values with dignity, fraternity and equality to attain prosperity in the society. In their foreword to International Documents on human rights compiled by Satish Chandra, G.V.G. Krishna Murthy states as a historical backdrop to the human rights struggle that "the first major statutory attempt in support of human rights against tyranny and arbitrary exercise of power by the sovereign could be traced to Magna Carta of 1215 A.D. in England followed by several; other statutes. The movements in favour of human rights remained as national movements for several years till the American Revolution in 1778 and French Revolution in 1789 which made the expression of 'Liberty, equality and fraternity' ring and reverberate in all corners of the earth, awakening messes to rise and assert their basic rights which are entitled by virtues of birth as human beings".

There are several declaration which have paiddue importance to the human rights and recognized them for a dignified life in the society. Out of these, universal declaration of human rights of 10th December 1948 is famous document and it is also known as UN Declaration of human rights. Being a signatory of UN Charter it has adopted these principle in the preamble of the Constitution.

The issue for discussion is why human rights not able to operationalised by the Indian Constitution which has been enshrined in the preamble of the Constitution as a basic document and what could be the possible actions towards realising this. The logic behind of our discussion is to identify the paradoxes and contradictions, both inherent and induced and also to locate the reasons for failure to implement them. Some of them are:

> Human rights in India are universal in nature but it failed to provide a relief to certain sections of the society because they are sociologically downtrodden or kept away from the mainstream of the society. hence these sections were denied assets like owning of a land and other properties. The paradox of the Indian society is monopolisation of public property by the small section and they continue to enjoy the same that led to unequal society. Thus, human rights have become the privileges of the privileged.

With the introduction of privatisation in the areas of education and health sector the government has slowly withdrawing from these sectors which are again impacted on the larger chunk of marginalised sections of the population who are mainly depends on the government services. Though the government has created huge institutional infrastructure but it unable to render their services to these sections which again paradox to think on the lines human rights. Those who can afford economically are served by these institutions in the private sector. Hence the very important of nature of basic human rights is to serve the masses children in educationally and health with effective manner for the majority of the poor.

In respect of the administrative and legal systems also, the poor and disadvantaged are denied for their legitimate rights and opportunities. The paradox is that the language of administrative transactions, the terminologies and procedures are beyond the reach of disadvantaged.

The nature of legal system in the country also denies the poor on legal matters and sometimes it is beyond their reach. It mostly facilitates the rich who are able pay the legal practitioners services at judiciary. In the case of the poor and marginalised sections the justice is always delayed rather than providing necessary relief to them.

In the case of rights related to economic development also the situation is similar. The paradox is that the schemes lunched for poor are not effectively implemented or sometimes not reaching to them. In majority cases, the poor and the marginal sections of the society are not involved in their own developmental paradigm.

The Missing links

The missing link in availing the human rights is the absence of advocacy. Most of the people in India are not aware of their basic rights. There is no sensitisation about the citizens rights. To became a full fledged citizen of a country, one need to know about their rights. The documents on human rights are not available in their own mother tongues or people language. In fact, these documents needs to the popularised for effectively way to empower the lower range of social groups by the NGO's and other civil rights organisations and individuals working at local level should also be available with then and able to bring awareness to all in the society.

The people in the unorganised sector are supposed to be informed first about their economic rights like minimum wages, fixed working hours etc Those in the organised sectors are highly organised in the form of associations/unions and are able to get their benefits.

- Reforms have brought the public under control over it which is monopolised and managed by the dominant and oppressive sections of the society. The reforms should enable the small groups and consumers to gain effective access to the market system on a fair principle basis. Right to fair price and fair value to their limited incomes are basic for the survival of the poor.

- Empowering and capacity building processes are missing to the disadvantaged to people participate effectively in the development process on the basis of equality at the planning implementation levels and in sharing the benefits of development.
- There is need to humanise the administrative, legal, economic and political systems. The system should be people friendly and pro poor.

Unless there is an all out effort with full commitment in bringing in radical reforms and changes on the lines above, there is no possibility for the poor and disadvantaged to enjoy their rights on the basis of equality, self-determination and human dignity which is the true spirit of human rights.

Roots Cause for Violence in Andhra Pradesh

The growing animosity between the dalits and the upper castes in rural Andhra must be looked at the post-1947 period of social transformation. The caste system in Andhra Pradesh has undergone a profound change in terms of forming a new social classes and their power relations. The traditional caste hierarchy closely corresponded to the broad class divisions within the rural Andhra. That is, the landlords and rich peasantry in Andhra are mostly drawn from among the non-Brahmin upper castes such as the Reddies, Kammas, Kapus, Velamas. While the poor peasantry, tenants and agricultural labourers belonged to the Dalit communities. In post-Independent India socio-economic development led to the decline of parasitic old absentee feudal landlord classes. They lost their predominant position and grip over the economy and polity. Such a decline was also due to the abolition of zamindari system and the shift of landholding from absentee landlords to cultivating peasantry, mainly belonging to the Reddies, Kammas, Kapus castes. Available evidence clearly indicates that during the post-1950 period the agrarian society of Andhra Pradesh witnessed the crystallisation of a progressive and dynamic peasant bourgeois class, which had taken the advantages of new economic opportunities like commercial farming, green revolution, growth of agro-based industrialisation, etc., and they have consolidated their position as a dominant socio-political class. The drastic decline and disintegration of absentee landlordism represented by old zamindars and Brahmin inamdars also paved the way for the consolidation of a dynamic rural rich in the countryside. In caste terms, most of the neorich "Kulaks" belonged to the dominant upper castes. It may be pointed out that the rich peasantry among Kammas could continue maintain and improve their economic position because of their attachment to land and the extraordinary care they took in agriculture. In areas where they are numerically dominant, they emerged as a dominant class in all sector of human life. Similarly, same as the case with Kapus and Reddis also.

The strategies for rural development pursued by the state government, like the cooperative credit system, Panchayati Raj institutions all have helped these rich peasantry class immensely to augment resources in mobilisation and accumulation. Possession of considerable land property and accumulation of the surplus land by these castes further intensified their rural richness and also the process of stratification within the peasantry, which resulted alienation of land by the lower castes and dalits. A recent study on labour relations in Andhra noted that "the proportion of the agricultural labourers in the total agricultural population had increased steadily and continuously from 27 per cent to 53 per cent between 1951 and 1981". Micro-level village studies of post-1960 period also revealed that a considerable section of the lower castes and Dalits do not posses any land. Thus, they constituted the rural poor in rural Andhra. Census data on caste and occupation indicates that the Mala and Madiga communities accounted for the bulk of the agricultural labour and working as farm/ field servants, palem and casual workers. The employment of the entire family (men, women) and children in the various agricultural operations is a unique feature of the Dalit communities.

The dominant upper caste, landowners thus exerted considerable power over the Dalits. In the villages majority of Dalits are agricultural labourers and poor peasants/tenants were dependent upon the rich Kamma and Reddy peasantry. Whenever the agricultural labourers demands the wage increase, they were subjected to the caste oppression like social boycott and denial of village economic resources. On the other the dominant rich peasantry also did not tolerate any upward mobility of the Dalits. Whenever these dalit families acquired a wasteland, housesites and other land grants from government the rich peasantry subjected to target to these Dalits by physical attack and invariably the demand for wage increase is always a rift between the rich and Dalits. This in -turn results a retaliation from the dominant caste in the form of abuse, harassment, molestation of women and destruction of property.

Even Dalits are easy targets for trivial accusations of theft and witchcraft. In these cases also there are number of incidences of caste discrimination incidents like of preventing their entry into temples, taking drinking water from public wells and tanks, denial of public utilities like hotels, barber shops etc. The growing assertion of Dalits in their articulation on the concept of citizenship, mass literacy is a basis for new civil life and their social mobility has invited them for victimisation by the dominant caste peasantry. The unabated caste violence against Dalits in the Andhra countryside is a proof of evidence.

Violation of Dalits rights

The violation of human rights situation in Andhra Pradesh remained a major cause of concerned for government in 2008. Both the security forces and the Maoists were responsible for gross violations human rights . During the period from January to May 2008, the Andhra Pradesh State Human Rights Commission (SHRC) received 439 cases of human rights violations against the police. SHRC chairperson Justice B. Subhashan Reddy stated that the SHRC received 5,392 human rights violation cases, including 89 cases of custodial torture, during 2007. Of them, 860 cases (15.9 per cent) were filed against the police.

In 2008, APSHRC documented a number of police custodial deaths in the state. These include the custodial death of Abdul Nabi at Chennur police station in Kadapa district on 3rd January 2008; Narsimhulu alias Anji Reddy in Devarakonda in Nalgonda district on 23rd March 2008; Nagaraju in Hindupur on 27th April 2008; Tamanaboni Ramulu in Devarakonda in Nalgonda district on 22nd May 2008; Nagula Ravinder Goud by the custody of the Excise Police in Husnabad in Karimnagar district on 11th August 2008; and of Meka Sankara Rao at Lalapet police station in Guntur district on 29 September 2008.

Caste Discrimination

Caste discrimination, social boycott and attacks on Dalits. On 21st June 2008, upper caste villagers attacked Dalits at Pottilanka village in Kadiyam mandal of East Godavari district and killed a Dalit named Palli Veerapandu. Human Rights Forum (HRF) fact-finding committee alleges that although the Dalits have given 50 names as attackers, the police could only arrested 29 people.

The two more incidents were occurred in the last decades of this century, wherein the assertion of the 'disable' has resulted in the elimination of the disabled by the abled. From Belchi to Karamchedu and Lakshmanpur Bathe to Chundur or Vempenta are many stories remain the same that the dominant castes intolerance to becomes caste attack on Dalits.

Let us study the incident of Tsundur, Tsundur is one of the big village in a coastal district of Guntur in Andhra Pradesh. This is a well developed village wherein the Tsundur, the mandal headquarter is located about 15 kms from Tenali town.

The most dominant castes are the Reddys with nearly 800 families, who also own most of the land. Among the scheduled castes, the largest group belongs to the Malas with nearly 4000 families while there are about 100 Madiga families. Unlike in other villages, the Dalits of Tsundur are better educated. Some of them even occupied the political positions. And good numbers of them are employed. On the other hand, members of the upper castes, particularly the Reddys and Telagas are less educated and most of the youth do hard labour like tractor drivers or are engaged in farming.

Enlightened by Dalits youth have begun challenge the upper castes. This was the cause of constant friction between the Dalits and the Upper castes. however they are educated they are far behind the upper castes, in all respects. Though their economically backward but they never surrendered to them rather they emerged as successful group politically. The Tsundur MPP is a Dalit. Dalits were also elected as MPPs of the adjacent mandals such as Amrutalur, Ponnur, Nagaram and Intur. All of these are reserved constituencies. Their political enlightenment has posed a challenge to the existing upper caste and they also felt that their dominance in the village was slowly being eroded.

In July 1989 in Vempenta village of Kurnool district. Brutally six Dalits were killed. Vempenta, a village in the Pamulapadu mandal in a faction ridden Rayalaseema region. Major chunk of the population are Dalits and backward class. Among the scheduled castes, the largest group is Madigas. Among backward community Gandla community is prominent in this village. Madiga youth have occupied the endowment land. They distributed the land to other groups also.

The self assertion of Dalits, however unpalatable to the landlords which led for a gang war on dalits. Political gangsterism and upper castes intolerance of Dalits self-assertion can be seen behind every incident of atrocities on Dalits.

The dominant castes leader led by Bomma Sivaiah wanted the endowment should be auctioned publicly. Mr. sivaiah has the support of ex -Atmakur MLA(Vengal ready). There was a feud between Swarna Pullaiah and Bomma Sivaiah belongs to Gandla community to establish their dominance in the village. Bomma Sivaiah was the root cause for the problem where he used his influence and prevented the Dalits from entering the occupied lands. So there was ensued a long drawn battle, where the militancy was only option but to advance their struggle in militant way. This resulted in the death of Sivaiah on July 15, 1998.

The landlords, who were just waiting for the chance, made all preparation and launched attacks on the Madigawada on the 15 night itself. Those who attacked Madigawada were all the followers of Vengal Reddy. Sivaiah and others. They brutal killings were continued till the 16th early hours upto 8 O' clock, where in nine people were killed. Among the killed there were six Dalits and there backward castes people. Those who were killed were thrown into the fire, leaving absolutely no evidence of the killings. They just not killed and they aroused and destroyed nearly 90 houses of the Dalits.

The incidents of Tsundur and Vempenta was not clearly demonstrates the killings it also highlight the close kinship or political ties in killing of dalits. The upper caste peasantry never wants dalit to attain or empower. These two incidents will narrates the relation between the rich and poor dalits in rural Andhra. Even at Chundur police were present at the spot but did nothing to prevent the assault. There even after the incidents the police had been equally lethargic.

The police never made any serious attempts to apprehend the principal assailants. Even if they make the arrest, the investigation was carried in a most causal manner (Resulting in the discharge of accused, the Karamchedu case as the best example.

In 2007, Andhra Pradesh ranked fourth worst in atrocities against Dalits. According to the NCRB, 3383 cases of crimes committed against Dalits were reported from Andhra Pradesh, representing 11.3 per cent of total such cases in India. These included 46 cases of killings, 105 cases of rape, 25 cases of abduction, 17 cases of arson, 122 cases registered under the Protection of Civil Rights Act of 1955 and 1200 cases registered under SC/ST (Prevention of Atrocities) Act of 1989, among others.

On 21 June 2008, upper caste villagers attacked Dalits at Pottilanka village in Kadiyam mandal of East Godavari district, and killed Palli Veerapandu. Human Rights Forum (HRF) fact-finding committee stated that a Dalit youth named Ambadi Rajaratnam was beaten up by Kapus (upper caste community) for allegedly having an the legal affair with a Kapu girl in the village. On the following day morning, when the youth went to the same hotel for breakfast, he was again beaten up. The HRF report stated that "Suspecting the Dalits would retaliate; the upper castes raided the area where the Dalits lived with lethal weapons, pelted stones and beat up whoever they came across. Palli Veerapandu died on the spot due to head injury, while Vemula Yesu was seriously injured and is still in Kakinada general hospital fighting for life." The HRF further stated that Dalits of the village specifically named 50 of the attackers but the police arrested only 29 persons. While former Mandal Parishad Territorial Constituency (MPTC) member Kothapalli Satyanarayana alias Chantibabu was named as having played a key role in the attack, police did not arrest him.

On the night of 21 August 2008, upper caste people attacked the Dalits at Kodavalapuri village in Kotavuratla mandal in Visakhapatnam district. The attacks were in retaliation to the boycott of the Dalits to perform the age-old ritual of pulling the "village goddess" chariot. The problem started after the upper caste villagers protested against serving of liquor to them in the same glasses used by Dalits. When the Dalits protested against discrimination and untouchability, upper caste people attacked them. During the attacks, the Dalits were dragged out of their homes and assaulted. The attackers attacked indiscriminately attacking pregnant women, old people and children. Despite this the police first filed a case against the Dalits following a complaint filed by the village vice-headman P. Govinda Rao. But following media coverage of the incident, on 24 August 2008 the police registered a case under the SCs/STs (Prevention of Atrocities Act against a number of upper caste people.

On 8 September 2008, Dalits staged protests against discrimination by upper caste villagers at Nelagonda village in Guntakal mandal in Anantapur district. The Dalits alleged that the upper caste villagers did not allow them to take out a procession as part of "Vinayaka Chaviti" celebrations. Following this, the upper caste people prevented Dalit students from attending the village school. In September 2008, as many as 11 Dalits belonging to three families sought the state Government's intervention against social boycott by the upper caste for the last three months at Kazigudem village under Pedapadu mandal in West Godavari district. The children from these three families were not allowed to go to the local government school and the local shopkeeper refused to sell goods to them. In July 2007, many villagers suffered losses due to floods. The district administration supplied relief material to 30 families who were affected. However, village elders issued an order saying that the relief material given by the government should be shared among all families in the village, whether or not they were affected by the floods. However, the family members of Mekathoti Naraiah, Kalaparthi Mariadas and Dasari Issac (all Dalits did not accept the decision of the village elders. And on 1 July 2008, the village elders imposed a fine of Rs 1,000 each on the three Dalit families. When the Dalit families failed to pay the fine, they were socially boycotted.

Violations of the rights of women

In 2007, Andhra Pradesh was also famous for crimes against women. In its latest report "Crime in India 2007", the NCRB stated *"Andhra Pradesh, accounting for nearly 7.2 per cent of the country's population, has accounted for 13.3 per cent of total incidents of crime against women in the country by reporting 24,738 cases."* The NCRB recorded 24,738 cases of crimes committed against women including

1,070 cases of rape, 1,564 cases of kidnapping and abduction, 613 cases of dowry deaths, 11,335 cases of domestic violence and 4,406 cases of molestation, among others. In terms of crimes against women, Hyderabad stands first with 1,931 cases was the second most unsafe city in India, next to Delhi (4,331 cases).

In 2007, the APWC registered 1,082 cases of violence against women in the state. It also registered 250 cases in 2008 up to 30 October 2008. As many as 1,227 cases were pending disposal as of November 2008.

SC man beaten to death

Namala in Anantapur district on March 31, 2011, two persons from dominant upper caste, by name Venkatrami Reddy and Narender Reddy, allegedly beaten a Scheduled Caste person, Tirupathi (30) who later succumbed to injuries.

According to Sub-Inspector K. Prasad of C.K. Palle police station, a minor scuffle had broken out between Tirupathi and the two persons from Namala village at a meeting organised by Revenue officials for disbursing 'Pattadhar' passbooks at Chennekothapalle village. The two persons allegedly beaten Tirupathi when he try to sit in the front row to collect his 'Pattadhar' passbook. Tirupathi, who sustained internal injuries, returned home and succumbed to 'severe pain'. When he was taken to the local hospital, the doctor said that he was already dead.

Finally, the caste based atrocities are still persisting in India, world's largest democracy despite of all legal safeguards, the vulnerable groups are not a position to enjoy their rights. The castebased discrimination is comfortably taking breath in a hierarchical society where the principle of graded inequality thus challenging the constitutional mandate of establishing an egalitarian social order. The ineffective implementation of the prevention of atrocities act, under-reporting of atrocities cases, along with the inherent vested interests in maintaining the caste discrimination, are the reasons for the perpetuating atrocities. Improper investigation on atrocities cases results in low conviction rates. According to the NHRC annual report 27, 894 cases were registered under the Atrocities Act in 2002 and only 2.31 per cent of cases were convicted. The low rate of convection i s a result of varying factors like caste bias by the prosecutors as well as other agencies of the government, including the judiciary and the law enforcement machinery's lack of familiarity with the provision of the relevant legislation. A check on the law enforcement machinery in this regard is much needed and requires legal scrutiny.

Majority of women from scheduled castes suffer from suppression and violation of human rights just because they don't have any support from civil society. In spite of constitutional guarantees, and other safeguards, scheduled caste women fail to enjoy the fruits of the Constitution. Most of the scheduled caste women, work in unorganised sector, where there is no security for employment as well security to their livelihood. This clearly indicates how badly the lower rung people are being exploited by the dominant and landlord communities in Andhra Pradesh. Good number of women lib organisations and non-governmental organisations trying their best to motivate the people who are suffering in the hands of upper caste people. Unless and until the civil society feels that the age old practice of bonded labour, caste discrimination and humiliation of lower castes be put to an end, and discontinue this morbid culture, nothing will be achieved in the direction of protective discrimination.

References

V. Eswara Reddy, Operationalisation of Human Rights in independent India – The Paradoxes and missing links.

Ibid.

Ibid.

Chandu Subba Rao, D. Francis, Development of weaker sections Rawat Publication, Jaipur and New Delhi.

Deccan Herald, August 5, 1958, cited in N.D.Kamble, "Atrocities on Scheduled castes", New Delhi, 1980, p. 32-33.

For an analysis of agrarian relation during the post-1947 period, A. Satyanarayana, "Caste and class in Rural Andhra: A Historical Perspectives", K.L. Sharma, (ed) caste and class in India, Jaipur, 1994, pp. 376-93.

AP cops biggest rights violators, The Deccan Chronicle, 27 May 2008.

Probe into custodial death, The Hindu, 5 January 2008.

Man dies in police custody at Devarakonda, The Hindu, 24 February 2008.

Man dies in police station at Hindupur, The Deccan Chronicle, 28 April 2008.

Accused dies in police station; kin stage protest, The Hindu, 23 May 2008.

Man dies in excise police lock-up, The Hindu, 12 August 2008.

Broker dies in police station, The Deccan Chronicle, 30 September 2008.

Pottilanka: HRF demands arrest of all the accused, The Hindu, 2 July 2008, available at http://www. hindu.com/2008/07/02/stories/2008070252470300. htm.

Sudhakar Pasala, State Dalits Human Rights – A study into Chundur and Vempenta Killings, 1998.

APCLC, "The Chundur Carnage" an APCLC Publication, Hyderabad, Aug, 1991. p. 5.

Ibid., p. 7.

Ilaiah, Kancha, "Vempentalo Jarigindi Manu Nyayam", DBMS Publication, Hyderabad, 1998, p. 136.

DBMS, "Vempenta Dalitwada Pai Dadi" DBMS Publication, August, 1998, Hyderabad.

Varavara Rao, "Vempenta lo Emi Jarigindi? Enduku Jarigindi" DBMS Publication, Hyderabad, 1998, p. 107.

2007 annual report of national crime records bureau, Govt of India.

Pottilanka: HRF demands arrest of all the accused, The Hindu, 2 July 2008.

Case booked for attack on dalits, The Hindu, 24 August 2008.

Village tense as Dalits stage stir, The Deccan Chronicle, 9 September 2008.

Dalits face boycott, The Deccan Chronicle, 30 September 2008.

2007 Annual Report of NCRB, Govt of India.

AP women's panel chief exposed in sting, Deccan Herald, September 15, 2007.

Women's panel in a mess, The Deccan Chronicle, 12 November 2008.

Women's panel to be revamped, The Hindu, 13 March 2008.

The Hindu, Thursday, March 31, 2011.

10

Ambedkar Views on Castes in India

— *M. Thangaraj*

Caste system segregates the people based on birth, each caste has its own traditional hereditary occupation. These castes were grouped into four categories, (*varna* system), viz., *Brahmins, Kshatriyas, Vaishyas,* and *Shudras*. The people who were excluded from the four fold *varna* system, and Untouchables or outcastes. Untouchable were prohibited from entering into temple and acquiring property. They were compelled to perform the menial and other low paid or inferior occupations. 'Their touch, shadow and even voices were deemed by the caste Hindus to be polluting.....They were denied the use of public wells and were condemned to drink any filthy water they could find.'[1] Even after 67 years of independence, discrimination faced by the Untouchables has not changed substantially. Caste system has not only penetrated into livelihood of the people, but also deeply entrenched into the politics. "In politics, caste is the most potent basis of mobilisation, no political party are even progressive one, can successfully contest an election without manipulating the caste arithmetic to its advantage."[2] "Hinduism is a menace to liberty, equality and fraternity. On that account it is incompatible with democracy. Hindu Raj must be prevented at any cost."[3] "Caste system is an institution of oppression and social discrimination. It is embedded in production relation and is an impediment to the growth of the productive forces, and a bulwark against revolutionary overthrow of the ruling classes."[4]

"The economic network of caste-based institutions are awesome. A huge number of hospitals, schools, colleges, cooperative banks and other modern institutions are controlled by thinly-veiled caste institutions."[5]

Ambedkar presented a paper on "Castes in India: Their Mechanism, Genesis and Development" at the seminar of A.A. Goldenweizer organised by the Department of Anthropology at Colombia University, New York in USA on 9th May 1916, when he was undergoing Doctoral Studies. He deals with this subject from Anthropological point of view. While discussing about the people of India, Ambedkar observed that "according to well-known ethnologists, the population of India is a mixture of Aryans, Dravidians, Mongolians and Scythians. All these stocks of people came to India from various directions with various cultures, centuries ago, when they were in tribal state."[6] They fought with their predecessors to ensure about their arrival. In the course of time, they lost their self-identity. Hence they evolved a common culture and, at the same time, they could not create a single culture for them.

Definition of Caste

Ambedkar examined four definitions of the caste propounded by the best scholars on this subject. They are: Senart, a French author, defines caste as "a close corporation, in theory at any rate rigorously hereditary; equipped with a certain traditional and independent organisation, including a chief and a council, meeting on occasion in assemblies of more or less plenary authority and joining together at certain festivals; bound together by common occupations, which relate more particularly to marriage and to food and to questions of ceremonial pollution, and ruling its members by the exercise of jurisdiction, the extent of which varies, but which succeeds in making the authority of the community more felt by the sanction of certain penalties and, above all, by final irrevocable exclusion from the group".

Nesfield defines caste as "a class of community which disowns any connection with any another class and can neither intermarry nor eat nor drink with any but persons of their own community".

Sir H. Risley defines caste as "a caste may be defined as a collection of families or groups of families bearing a common name which usually denotes or is associated with specific occupation, claiming common descent from a mythical ancestor, human or divine, professing to fallow the same professional callings and are regarded by those who are competent to give an opinion as forming a single homogeneous community".

Katkar defines caste as "a social group having two characteristics: (i) Membership is confined to those who are born of members and includes all persons so born; (ii) The members are forbidden by an inexorable social law to marry outside the group".

Ambedkar reviewed the definitions given by these four scholars and found that authors of the definitions are discussed too much or too little; these definitions were incomplete or incorrect and all of them have missed the central point in the mechanism of the caste system. Their mistake lies in trying to define caste system as an isolated unit and not as a group within.

Nature of Caste

Having discussed about the definition of the term 'caste' Ambedkar tried to explain the nature or characteristics of the caste. Mr. Senart draws attention to the "idea of pollution" as characteristics of caste. Ambedkar did not accept with Senart and he viewed that the idea of pollution is by no means a peculiarity to caste as such. Ambedkar further stated that the idea of pollution usually originates in priestly ceremonialism and is a case of general belief in purity. He concluded that the "idea of pollution" is a characteristic of caste only in so far as caste has a religious flavour.[7]

Mr. Nesfield dwells on the absence of messing with those outside the caste as one of its characteristics. Ambedkar viewed that caste being self enclosed unit naturally limits social intercourse, including messing etc. to members within it. Consequently this absence of messing with outsiders is not due to positive prohibition, but is a natural result of caste, i.e. exclusiveness. No doubt this absence of messing originally due to exclusiveness, acquired the prohibitory character of a religious injunction, but it may be regarded as a later growth.

With respect to Katkar's definition, there is a slight confusion of thought, lucid and clear as otherwise it is. He speaks of prohibition of intermarriage and membership by autogeny as the two characteristics of caste. Ambedkar stated that these two aspects are one and the same thing, and not two different things. If you prohibit intermarriage the result is that you limit membership to those born with in the same group. Thus, the two are the obverse and the reverse sides of the same model.[8]

Thus, the critical analysis clearly brings out that prohibition or absence of intermarriage – endogamy is only one that can be called the essence of caste. Ambedkar stated that the peoples of India form a homogeneous whole. The various races of India occupying definite territories have more or less fused into one another and do posses cultural unity, which is the only criterion of a homogeneous population. Ambedkar concluded that "caste in India means an artificial chopping off the population into fixed and definite units, each one prevented from fusing into another through the custom of endogamy."[9]

Creation of Caste

Ambedkar viewed that the exogamy was practiced in the primitive world. With the growth of history, the exogamy lost its efficacy. With the exogamy as the rule there could be no caste, for exogamy means fusion. Endogamy is foreign to the people of India.

But now we have caste, which means the super position of endogamy on exogamy. Ambedkar explained with an example as how the caste was created. If a group desires to make itself endogamous a formal injunction against intermarriage with outside group, it is absolutely necessary to circumscribe a circle outside which people should not contract marriages.[10]

A group desirous of making itself into a caste, the maintenance of equality between the sexes becomes the ultimate goal, for without it, endogamy will not subsist. In other words, if endogamy is to be preserved conjugal rights from within have to be provided for, otherwise members of the group will be driven out of the circle to take care themselves in any way they can.[11]

Absolute parity between the sexes is impossible to maintain. The parity will be realised only when couple dies simultaneously. But this is rare contingency. The husband may die before the wife and create a surplus woman, who must be disposed of; else through intermarriage she will violate the endogamy of the group. Likewise wife may die before the husband and create a surplus man. Thus, both the surplus man and surplus woman constitute a menace to the caste if they don't find suitable partners inside the prescribed circle. Hence they are likely to transgress the boundary, marry outside and import offspring that is foreign to the caste.[12]

1. A surplus woman

Ambedkar states that surplus woman (widow) can be disposed of in two different ways so as to preserve the endogamy of the caste. First, burn her on the funeral pyre of her deceased husband and get rid of her. If she is not disposed of, she may marry outside the caste and violate endogamy or she may marry within the caste and through competition encroach upon the chances of marriage that must be reserved for the potential brides in the caste. She is therefore a menace in any case. The second remedy is to enforce widowhood on her for the rest of her life. She can be degraded to a condition in which she is no longer a source of allurement.[13]

2. A surplus man

From time immemorial man has upper hand as compared to woman. He is dominant figure in every group and of the two sexes has greater prestige. With this traditional superiority of man over woman his wishes have always been consulted. The project of burning along with his wife is hazardous in two ways viz. 1. It can't be done, simply because he is a man. 2. If done, a sturdy soul is lost to the caste. Here he has two options viz. 1. He has to follow self imposed celibacy, 2. He may be provided with wife only by recruiting a bride from the ranks of those not yet marriageable in order to tie him down to the group. Thus, there are four ways in which numerical disparity between the two sexes is conveniently maintained. They are: (1) burning the widow with her deceased husband; (2) compulsory widowhood - a milder form of burning; (3) imposing celibacy on the widower and (4) wedding him to a girl not yet marriageable.

Mechanism (of the creation and preservation of Caste)

The Hindu society presents three singular uxorial customs, namely: 1. Sati or burning of the widow on the funeral pyre of her deceased husband. 2. Enforced widowhood by which a widow is not allowed to remarry. 3. Girl marriage. On the part of widower *sannyasa* (renunciation) is the custom. Ambedkar is of the view that there is no scientific explanation on the origin of these customs even today. Sati has been honoured because it is a "proof of the perfect unity of body and soul" between husband and wife and of "devotion beyond the grave", because it embodied the ideal of wifehood, which is well expressed by *Uma* when she said, "Devotion to her lord is woman's honour, it is her eternal heaven; she further states that "I desire not paradise itself if thou are not satisfied with me!" Ambedkar stated that he did not get anyone who has praised, although there were many who adhered to it. A faithful man or woman ought not to feel affection for woman or man other than the one whom he or she united. Such purity is compulsory not only after marriage but even before marriage, this is known as chastity. Even a girl should not be considered pure, if she loves a man before her marriage. If she does so, it is a sin hence girl's marriage. "Sati, enforced widowhood and girl marriages are customs that were primarily intended to solve the problem of the surplus man and surplus woman in a caste and to maintain its endogamy. Strict endogamy could not be preserved without these customs, while caste without endogamy is a fake."[14]

Growth and Spread of Caste System

There are two ways by which the institution of caste spread among the non-Brahmin population, viz. 1. Caste system has either been imposed upon the docile population of India by law giver as a divine dispensation, or 2. It has grown according to some law of social growth peculiar to India. As far as the point one is concerned, Manu, the lawgiver of India could not have been invented the caste system. He must have codified the existing rules and preached the caste dharma.

The question whether the Brahmins created the caste, imposing the caste system on the non-Brahmin population was beyond their mettle. They would have helped the process by their glib philosophy, but they certainly could not have pushed their scheme beyond their own confines.[15]

The orthodox Hindus believe that the Hindu society was created by the *Shastras*. According to Ambedkar, the Hindu society is composed of classes viz.

1. *Brahmins* or the priestly class;
2. The *Kshatriya* or the military class;
3. The *Vaishya* or the merchant class; and
4. The *Shudra* or the artisan and menial class.

This system was essentially a class system, in which individuals, when qualified, could change their class. At the same time the priestly class socially detached itself from the rest of the people and through a closed door policy became a caste by itself. The other social classes being subjected to law of social division of labour underwent differentiation, some into large, others into very minute groups.[16]

Imitation and the Basis for Formation of Caste

Ambedkar explained the creation of caste with psychological interpretation. Endogamy or closed-door system was a fashion in the Hindu society, and as it had originated from the Brahmin caste and it was whole-heartedly imitated by all the non-Brahmin sub-divisions or classes, who in their turn became endogamous castes. It is "the infection of imitation" that caught all these sub-divisions on their onward march of differentiation and has turned them into castes.

Ambedkar explains 'the laws of imitation' as given by Gabriel Trade. They are: 1. Imitation flows from the higher to the lower; 2. The extent or intensity of imitation varies inversely in proportion to distance.

Ambedkar enumerated two conditions for imitations. They are: 1. The sources of imitation must enjoy prestige in the group and 2. There must be "numerous daily relations" among members of the group.

Ambedkar argued that these conditions were present in India. The Brahmin is a semi-god very nearly a demi-god. He sets up a mode and moulds the rest. Observation of the customs of sati, enforced widowhood, and girl marriage varies in the Hindu society. Observation of these customs varies directly with the distance that separates the caste. Those castes that are nearest to the Brahmins have imitated all the three customs and insist on the strict observance. Those that are less near have imitated enforced widowhood and girl marriage; others a little further off, have only girl marriage and those furthest off have imitated only the belief in the caste principle. The above analysis shows that non-Brahmin class became castes on the pattern of the Brahmin caste.

Mechanistic Process of the Formation of Caste

There are some classes who closed their doors, which resulted in being closed out. Ambedkar called this process as mechanistic process of caste. He says that caste in the singular number is an unreality. Castes exist only in the plural number. There is no such thing as a caste; there are always castes.

Now let us examine the self-duplication of caste as a result of fissiparous character of caste. Any innovation that seriously antagonises the ethical, religious and social code of the caste is not likely to be tolerated by the caste, and the recalcitrant members of a caste are in danger of being thrown out of the caste. Thus, the excommunicated members form themselves into new castes.

To sum up, Ambedkar has observed that 'several mistakes committed by the students of castes, which have misled them in their investigations'. Ambedkar further stated that they also could not explain how occupational groups became caste groups. Ambedkar's study on caste problem has four main points, viz. 1. That in spite of the composite make-up of the Hindu population, there is a deep cultural unity; 2. That caste is a parcelling into bits of a larger cultural unity; 3. That there was one caste to start with and 4. That classes have become castes through imitation and excommunication.[17] He viewed that he has given a scientific explanation about the castes in India. He exhorted that "the car has been shunted on wrong lines, and the primary object of the paper is to indicate what I regard to be the right path of investigation, with a view to arrive at a serviceable truth. We must, however, guard against approaching the subject with a bias. Sentiments must be outlawed from the domain of science and things should be judged from an objective standpoint."[18] He concluded his analysis by stating that "I am ambitious to advance a Theory of Caste, it can be shown to untenable, I shall be equally willing to give up."[19] Thus, Ambedkar's views on the question of castes are based on scientific approach and he made an impeccable contribution to the problem of castes in India.

Notes

1. Dhananjay Keer, *Ambedkar: Life and Mission,* Popular Prakashan, Mumbai, 2012, p. 1.
2. Lancy Fernandes and Satyajit Bhatkal, *The fractured civilisation: Caste society in the throes of change,* Bharatiya Janwadi Agahdi, Mumbai, 1999, p. 4.
3. Babasaheb Ambedkar Writings and Speeches", Vol. 8, Government of Maharashtra, Bombay, 1990, p. 358.
4. Ramachandran and Madhura Swaminathan, *Dalit households in village economies,* Tulika Books, New Delhi, 2014.
5. Lancy Fernandes and Satyajit Bhatkal, *Op.cit.*, p. 5.
6. Babasaheb Ambedkar Writings and Speeches, Vol.1, Government of Maharashtra, Bombay, 1979, p. 6.
7. Babasaheb Ambedkar Writings and Speeches, *ibid,* p. 7.
8. Babasaheb Ambedkar Writings and Speeches, *ibid,* p. 8.
9. Babasaheb Ambedkar Writings and Speeches, *ibid,* p. 9.
10. Babasaheb Ambedkar Writings and Speeches, *ibid,* pp. 9-10.
11. Babasaheb Ambedkar Writings and Speeches, *ibid,* p. 10.
12. Babasaheb Ambedkar Writings and Speeches, *ibid,* p. 10.
13. Babasaheb Ambedkar Writings and Speeches, *ibid,* p. 10.
14. Babasaheb Ambedkar Writings and Speeches, *ibid,* p. 14.
15. Babasaheb Ambedkar Writings and Speeches, *ibid,* p. 16.
16. Babasaheb Ambedkar Writings and Speeches, *ibid,* pp. 17-18.
17. Babasaheb Ambedkar Writings and Speeches, *ibid,* p. 22.
18. Babasaheb Ambedkar Writings and Speeches, *ibid,* p. 22.
19. Babasaheb Ambedkar Writings and Speeches, *ibid, p.22.*

11

Understanding the Origins of Inequality: People and their Access to Means of Development

— *C. Jerome Samraj*

Introduction

The process of modern development in India was origin in the colonial period as the colonial government established several institutions for governance including various departments and its offices at the presidency, district and sub-district (Taluk) levels, and infrastructures such as schools, roadways and railways. All these collectively produced an urban space that was very different from the traditional urban centres of the pre-colonial era, which were mostly religious / pilgrimage centres.[1] While the traditional temple urbanism were characterised by rigid caste structure and caste-based occupations. The urban centres that emerged during the colonial period had very distinct features, and it created a need for manual labour to construct its new offices, lay roads and railway tracks, and to render several services in the newly emerging offices. While people belonging to the 'upper' castes that had access to education by then got employment opportunities in colonial government offices, people who were placed lower in the social order, did not get such access.[2] However, the larger socio-economic changes due to establishment of colonial government, together with natural disasters like flood, drought and famine resulted in large scale starvation that necessitated government intervention. Colonial government devised food-for-work programmes to engage the poor in public works in order to enable them to survive famine. Such programmes provided a possibility for migration to the oppressed lower Shudra and 'Untouchable' castes to engage in labouring and service occupations that were emerging in that period.[3]

Development in post-independent India solely depended on the role of modern institutions established by colonial government. While the rigid caste-based Indian society provided no scope for socioeconomic mobility, the development process that unfurled due to establishment of a modern government and its various administrative offices, establishment of education system, evolution of new urban spaces which could provide a safety of anonymity for the 'untouchable' castes, provided the possibility of earning a livelihood from occupations other than traditional caste-based occupations. While the traditional social structure determined one's occupation at birth, and offered no chance of mobility, evolution of modern occupations facilitated opportunities based on criteria such as eligibility and skill, thereby created the possibility of relieving individuals from burdens of his / her caste. This had socio-economic impacts of varying significance on members of different castes across the social hierarchy, and since then, development turned out to be a process of people moving away from traditional caste-based occupations and entering jobs provided by the changing society. This paper attempts to draw an overview of how the unequal social foundations continue to reconfigure into multiple inequalities that simultaneously contribute in making the development process a rigid unequal reality.

This article attempts to understand the structural inequalities that determined people's access to productive resources, education, employment, and how the structural inequalities in these very means of development made development an unequal process. The following section of this article would map out how village and caste has determined people's access to means of development.

Village, Caste and People's Access to Development

While the modern development process opened up a wide range

of opportunities, people's ability to shift from traditional occupations to new ones was determined by a set of factors such as their position in the caste structure and the resultant access to productive assets, access to education and the duration of such access,[4] access to modern institutions and government, the relative levels of urbanisation and transportation that determined migration, etc.With this, consider a typical village, the population will be divided into different into castes and socio-economic and cultural rights of people were determined by the relative position of their castes in the scale of ritual purity and pollution. Membership of caste was restricted to birth which in turn restricted socioeconomic mobility of each individual. Brahmins, being a 'high and pure' caste remain at the top of the hierarchy, followed by non-brahmin 'upper' castes with relatively lesser privileges, followed by artisans such as goldsmiths, carpenter, blacksmiths, sculptor, potters and weavers - both silk and cotton, the lower *Shudra* castes who were involved in agriculture as landless agricultural workers, and service castes such as barbers and washermen, followed by 'untouchable' castes, who are currently listed as Scheduled Castes. If there are multiple castes among the Scheduled Castes, these castes are also hierarchically placed based on the notions of ritual purity and pollution and are forced into menial and de-humanising occupations. All these makes to the village as a source of productive resources and as a social space, where different castes are coordinated in the agrarian production process.

In a period when other sectors had not developed, land was the only productive resource and caste system had determined people's access to land and the nature of such access. The right to control land was bestowed upon castes that were 'ritually high and pure' and all other castes of the village had to settle for inferior socio-cultural and economic status depending upon their ritual status. The ideology of ritual purity and pollution condemned physical labour which is unavoidable integral to agrarian production processes as demeaning and inferior and the most unproductive work in the agrarian world - the priesthood is not only superior but also sacred. This socio-religious hierarchy also reflected on the system of remuneration, as the high and pure castes were given the highest respect and retained the agrarian surplus as their property, whereas other castes were forced to work as labourers for very meagre remuneration. Especially the labourers belonging to 'untouchable' castes and the service castes were given left over food as remuneration for their labour, which means they do not have no other choice than to come for work from dawn to dusk. People were subjected to varying levels of restrictions on occupations, sociocultural and religious rights and spatial mobility within the village. All these collectively made the village a space of multidimensional inequalities.

It can be ascertained from the works of historians that the village structure has remained the same for major part of history. If we took at the history of Tamil Nadu, this unchanging village structure can be understood from the fact that historian Karashima has used F.W. Ellis's papers on Mirasi Rights written in the early decades of nineteenth century to interpret the social structure from the inscriptions belonging to ninth and tenth centuries.[5] This means that village social structure and its socio-cultural system of rights and denials has remained unaltered until the advent of colonial period. And the colonial establishment which is the foundation of modern economic development process has been built on this social structure.

While the colonial government was establishing several offices all through the region, people's interaction with colonial state was moderated by the local social structure, and the first to get in touch with the colonial administration were the Brahmins. On the one side, the East India Company needed the recognition of the local power structure in order to establish control, and on the other side, the sections locally powerful needed the recognition of the colonial powers to retain their hegemony.

In this context, the control over local society enabled Brahmin and Vellalas castes the proximity to colonial powers and they were employed in the offices of Madras Presidency in various capacities. Their presence in local offices of colonial government not only moderated colonial policy-making, it also determined its reach to the rest of the society.[6] Owing to the proximity to the colonial offices, the people at the top of the social order were informed about policy changes much ahead of the rest of the society. Sometimes, they were also part of the policy-making processes, but for communities that were placed lower got access to this with a significant time lag, which contributed in inter-caste socio-cultural inequalities reconfigure into rigid disparities among the people. This can be understood if we analyses the evolution of colonial land revenue policies where the initial set of policies approved all the traditional socio-cultural rights of the 'high and pure' castes. As a result all the fertile wet lands of the villages became the property of the 'high and pure' castes and all the other castes placed below became landless agricultural labourers. While all the fertile lands of the villages had already become the private property of 'high and pure' castes during the early decades of nineteenth century, it was only during the 1840s the colonial government realised that these castes have effectively denied the lower castes from access to land and it was only during 1890's that the colonial government realised the Depressed Classes being completely excluded from land ownership, after that they made conditional assignment of lands to these communities.[7] By then all the cultivable village lands had become private properties of either the 'high and pure' castes or the lower shudra castes, and no lands were left for the Depressed Classes. Thus, the local social structure has effectively determined the access to newly emerging state system and thereby determined people's access to modern rights including right to property.

People and their access to Education

While this has been the history of land revenue policies, the spatial discrimination in villages and the location of state offices will help us enunciate exclusion in other spheres. Consider a typical village comprising of ritually 'high and pure' castes, intermediary castes, carpenters and potters, the service castes such as barbers and washer men and the Scheduled Castes and the cultivable lands are controlled by 'high and pure' castes and intermediary castes to a limited extent. The residential areas are segregated based on castes with underlying notions of 'touchability' and 'untouchability'. Residential areas of 'touchable' castes would form the village centre, and the residential areas of castes that are treated untouchable will be located at a distance. Village becomes a restricted social space where spatial mobility of people are restricted by notions of 'ritual purity and pollution' of castes. While every caste other than the ritually 'high and pure' Brahmins faced restrictions of varying degree, the 'untouchable' castes were subjected to worst forms of discrimination that restricted their entry into main village. In this context, when the colonial government expanded its offices, only the residential areas of the 'high and pure' castes had the space to accommodate such offices. Therefore, the government offices, schools, post-office, etc would be located in residential area of 'high and pure' castes, which people belonging to 'lower' castes cannot access. Even today, the panchayat offices, ration shops, schools, cooperative banks, water tanks, library, etc, everything would be located in the main village. While these services provided by the government are meant to cater to people of all castes, practice of untouchability within the village determines whether these very facilities can be access by all. Therefore, the 'lower' castes, especially the Dalits, were prevented from easy and equal access to these services.

Since education is the process that enables people to shift to new occupations, unequal access to education also determined the people's access to employment and its nature. The socio-economically dominant 'upper' castes got early access to education and had diversified their families occupations, whereas the communities and families with minimal access to land has not been able to facilitate their children's education and hence continue to remain in their traditional occupations. Socio-economic independence of the parents determine whether they are able to send their children to school and till what level. Similarly, quality of education also differs across regions, rural and urban areas and the socio-economic and cultural atmosphere has a decisive influence on peoples approach to education, and what purpose does education serves them. The rich and poor do not have equal access to schooling and the quality of schools also varies across rural and urban areas.

Schools under the existing system can be categorised as State board government schools with vernacular medium of instructions, government schools and aided schools with English as medium of instruction, private matriculations schools, central schools like Kendriya Vidyalaya or Navodhaya, or ICSE and Anglo-Indian schools. It doesn't need much research to understand children from which socio-economic, and familial background would gain admission in which of these aforementioned schools. The quality of teaching, infrastructure, method of teaching, teachers' treatment of children, differs to a greater extent across these schools. Therefore, one cannot assume that children who have enrolled in schools have equal access to education.

In addition to the differences that arise out of structural / infrastructural factors, the experiential factors play a crucial role in forming the aspirations and attitude of the children. In a caste-based society, children belonging to different castes are not treated equally by the teachers and hence the educational experiences are also not equal for all the children in school. Our society has not evolved to a situation where a son or daughter of a poor casual labourer or a Dalit sanitation worker be treated equally as they treat the children of a government officer, or a dominant caste landlord, or a businessmen. Similarly, children of service castes like barber or washermen also face similar inferior treatment by the schooling system. A child may come across a situation where his/her parents are treated trivially without much respect whereas the parents who are placed higher in the socioeconomic or administrative ladder may not experience this. Similarly, children from these diverse social locations are not punished equally by the teachers in case of mistakes or indiscipline. We also frequently come across instances where the children are punished for their parent's inability to pay the fees in time, and Dalit children being forced to clean toilets or not allowed to take food in the noon-meal scheme or served at a different place, and so on. We have also come across several instances across the country where the caste-Hindus opposed noonmeals at schools being cooked by Dalits, and what would such schools mean to Dalit children. All these clearly indicate that the development planning has not been able to ensure an egalitarian schooling experience for children across the socio-economic background even for a single day, and these differential treatments have very serious implications on children's presence in school, their interest and aspirations and their educational attainment.

In case of higher education, there are government, aided and private arts and science colleges, government and private engineering colleges, deemed-to-be universities, state universities, central universities, IITs and IIMs and research institutes. This essentially replicates the social hierarchy, as the IIT and IIMs are provided with extremely sophisticated infrastructure, followed by the Central Universities, State Universities and the colleges. While there is a graded inequality in the salaries paid to teachers in apex institutions and other institutions, the rural institutions end up with demotivated and unaspiring teachers, unless the qualified individual sacrifices lucrative and sophisticated career opportunities in the apex institutes to teach the poor and rural. This difference contributes towards a very serious difference in the quality of teaching, infrastructure and learning experience which has a decisive impact on the students' abilities and their aspirations.

Further, when close to 70 per cent of the children study in vernacular medium, all the higher education institutions function with English as the medium of instruction, and most institutions do not provide any foundation course in English. Given the unequal schooling experiences, it is not difficult to understand students from which schooling, familial and socio-economic background would gain admission in these institutions. Further, after gaining admissions, students from relatively poor socio-economic and educational background have to compete with their counterparts from better schooling background. Students from twelve years of English medium training and from that of vernacular medium are taught in English, and all the students are expected to write their examination in English. As a result, students' difficulty with English weakens their performance in other papers, and it is very common to come across students committing suicides in higher education as they tend to accumulate arrears.[8] As a result, such suicides are always reduced as an outcome of underperformance and the process that leads to suicide is seldom examined.[9] Those students who manage to survive and pass out with relatively lesser grades continue to face difficulties in finding a proper employment.

Employment

The development process in India can be understood as the movement of people from rigid caste-based traditional occupations to modern occupations. Emergence of alternative occupations in a particular region is determined by the natural resources, and it can be discerned by looking at the pattern of industrialisation and urbanisation in India that the occupational diversity in the drier regions are relatively higher than the districts with better access to irrigation where agriculture still remains the primary occupation. While agriculture is the only productive occupation, caste system which centralises land control in favour of the 'high and pure' castes makes the lower castes dependent on the 'upper' castes for their livelihood, and this dependence in turn makes the dominant castes to exercise complete hegemony over the castes placed below. As a result, the people belonging to the oppressed castes realise working as agricultural wage labour as a sign of enslavement and hence look for every opportunity to move away from agriculture. Breaking their dependence on the dominant castes in the village is indeed an act of assertion, as they are no more under the control of the dominant castes. This process is facilitated when there is a higher the level of industrialisation and urbanisation as it increases the possibility of people moving away from traditional occupations, thereby results in the weakening of hierarchical socio-cultural and economic bondage within the village. It is based on this Vijayabaskar argues that the emergence of non-farm sector and the increasing casual labourers in it has economically liberated the 'lower castes from remaining as agricultural workers' (Vijayabaskar, 2010).

In addition to that, migratory tendency of the people has to be treated in the same manner, as possibility of migration is determined by the set of skills one possess, emergence of alternative sources of livelihood and social network. Development of transport network plays a significant role in determining the ability of a person to migrate – whether a person commutes to work or shifts residence from one place to another for the sake of it. Further, urban space is also plagued by attitudes of caste and religion based discrimination which decisively determines one's ability to find new employment. Structurally, people who are relatively affluent can migrate easily compared to the poor owing to two factors. Firstly, the possibility of the affluent sections possessing / acquiring the required set of skills is much high than the underprivileged and poor. And on the same note, one needs support by way of financial backing, accommodation, guidance, and proper network to get a suitable employment, and the oppressed sections face both structural disadvantages as they will be unable to migrate on their own risking their livelihood and the difference in the set of skills leave them discriminated in the job market.[10]

In addition to the factors discussed above, people's access to governance has been moderated by the local social hierarchy, and education has also been determined by the same. If we relate the development process with that of people's access to education, emergence of colonial offices also created the need for service occupations which became the scope for the labouring 'lower' shudra and 'untouchable' castes to earn a livelihood away from their traditional occupations. Urbanisation process and increasing density of populations created the need for service occupations such as washermen and barber. While these occupations are treated to be 'polluting and inferior' and hence lowly, these services are nevertheless essential. Higher density of population also meant increasing social anonymity and weakening of casteist socio-cultural relationships, and hence relatively more liberating space than their natives. Scope for higher and regular income and weakening social subordination influence migration of these service castes to the urban places. Hence these castes did not have to switch to new occupations but they could earn a more regular income without being subjected to traditional caste-based control as in villages. Even though in the recent years very modern beauty parlours and saloons have emerged were some have received formal training and an insignificant numbers of members of other castes have come into these occupations, whereas these continue to be caste-based occupation to a very large extent.

While the experience of barbers and washermen have been this, the experience of other communities including Dalits and lower shudra castes have been very different, as they had to shift to new occupations and this has been determined by their access to education, assets, and other endowments. With the formal sector being as low as five per cent of the economy, people with relatively lesser education depend only on the non-farm employment for their livelihood. And their resource endowments determine whether they shift as self-employed or as labourers, and what kind of occupations they shift to.While the urban areas provided an increased scope for formal employment for a small section of people who had completed higher secondary schooling, but a vast majority of them depend on unskilled or semi-skilled occupations, and casual labour as a source of livelihood. One other factor which contributes in this process is their family's asset holding which facilitates access to formal credits and enables them to become self-employed / entrepreneurs, and caste networks are very crucial social capital that facilitates this process. There can be two inferences, firstly, unequal schooling and collegiate education ensure that the children from Dalits and services castes like barber and washermen are relatively less skilled than their counterparts from other social sections. Secondly, the process of unequal skill formation has made the traditional occupation as their refuge as other social sections keep away from these occupations.

Moving away from these traditional occupation also depends upon the emergence of alternative sources of livelihood. A plethora of studies have established that the socio-economic conditions determines one's access to education and thereby determine the pattern of occupational diversification.[11] While construction of dams and the introduction of high yielding variety seeds during green revolution benefited the farmers, the industrialisation during the 1970's and 1980's generated a wide variety of 'easy entry and low remuneration' jobs. For example, industries like matchbox and fireworks, leather industries, handloom, dying, spinning mills, textiles and knitwear industries provided a wide range of 'easy entry and low remuneration' jobs. Apart from this, the increasing urbanisation and development of transport network created a larger demand for casual labour like construction works, and other works like electrician, plumber, automobile mechanics, etc. These became the scope for people with relatively lesser education or even for those who completed vocational and technical education.

Post-reforms industrialisation has also created a wide variety of jobs, but these jobs required formal degrees, which means that only those sections with bachelors or master's degree, or those with engineering degrees could apply for most of these firms. Apart from these formal positions, these firms also needed a wide range of services like gardening, housekeeping, canteens, and other such jobs. However, these jobs are essential for the everyday functioning of these firms, are kept informal and the workers for these works are hired through contractors, and are not direct employees of the firms. Thus, however regular the employment may be for these people, these jobs are highly insecure and uncertain.

One other very crucial aspect of industrialisation before 1980's is that, this was facilitated by the state, and most of these firms were public sector and these firms have been distributed across the districts and states. The state governments also encouraged industrialisation by establishing industrial estates across the districts, and it increased employment opportunities in every region. But, starting from 2000 onwards, the post-globalisation industrialisation has led to concentration of industries in a few metropolitan cities, and a vast majority of these firms are concentrated in six cities namely, Delhi, Mumbai, Kolkata, Chennai, Bengaluru and Hyderabad.[12] All these jobs required higher education and high level of specialisation in the respective fields, in addition to English language skills. It is common to observe that professionals from all across the country have now moved into these occupations, and each of these cities have become home for youth from various linguistic and regional background.This phenomena can be understood by relating the inequalities in the education system with the necessary qualifications for the jobs. Given the unequal schooling structure, these employment become easily attainable for children from English medium schooling and those who could compete the essential qualifying degrees with relatively higher grades. The fact that the larger metropolitan cities now have a multi-lingual and multiethnic populations working in these firms is an outcome of structural inequalities in education that extends into employment.

Conclusion

This paper attempted to map out the unequal nature of the development process. While the post-independent India marched towards a planned development process, the development outcome proves that the structural inequalities continues to play a decisive role in determining people's access to development. The preceding discussion based on village social structure and the resultant access to government and means of development proves that the development process is far from being equal. With education being the only route to escape traditional caste based occupation, the structural inequalities in schooling and collegiate education facilitates a process where the socioeconomic and cultural inequalities gets reconfigured into unequal skill formation across the students different schooling background.

Differences in curriculum, training and quality of schooling and the fee structures across schools and the resultant unequal access together determine one's ability to compete in the job market. This has determined the pattern of occupational diversification as people belonging to privileged castes had better access to land got education decades before other castes of their villages could access school and have landed in higher levels of employment. Similarly, access to urban space and the nature of such access, together with development of transport networks determined people's ability to diversify into new occupations. The fact that castes and its embedded socio-cultural and economic inequalities have been the single major determinant of people's access to development. And even if the existing systems become inclusive and are free from discrimination, the already established structures would continue to produce unequal development outcomes. The insensitivity of the school and collegiate curriculum, administrative systems, and the innate antagonistic attitude against the 'lower' castes, especially Dalits would continue to reconfigure caste and produce new forms of inequalities. Thus, inclusive and egalitarian development process becomes a distant dream.

Bibliography

Ahuja, Ravi: 'Labour Unsettled: Mobility and Protest in Madras region, 1750-1800', *The Indian Economic and Social Histoy Review*, Vol. 35, No. 4. 1998.

Basu, Rajsekhar: 'Investigating the Pariahs Right over 'waste': The Tussle between the Reformist and Conservative Bureaucracy in late Nineteenth Century Tamil Nadu', *Contemporary India,* Vol. 3, No. 3, 2004.

Bhaduri, Amit: "Development or Developmental Terrorism?" *Economic and Political Weekly*, 2007: 552-553.

Breman, Jan: "A Dualist Labour System? A Critique of the 'Informal Sector' Concept, II: A Fragmented Labour Market." *Economic and Political Weekly*, 1976: 1905-1908.

Breman, Jan: "A Dualistic Labour System? A Critique of the 'Informal Sector' Concept, I. Informal Sector." *Economic and Political Weekly*, 1976: 1870-1876.

Breman, Jan: "An Informalised Labour System: End of Labour Market Dualism." *Economic and Political Weekly*, 2001: 4804-4821.

Debaranjan: Is struggle for Livelihood a Criminal Offence?*Economic and Political Weekly* 2008: 19-22.

Heitzman, James: "Temple Urbanism in Medieval South India." *Journal of Asian Studies 46 (4)*, 1987.

Heitzman, James: "Urbanisation and Political Economy in Early South India: Kancipuram During the Cola period." In *Structure and Soceity in Early South India*, by Kenneth Hall. New Delhi: Oxford University Press, 2001.

"Help the Rich, Hurt the Poor: Case of Special Economic Zones" *Economic and Political Weekly,* 2007: 1900-1902.

Hjejle, Benedicte: "Slavery and Agricultural Bondage in South India in the Nineteenth century." *The Scandinavian Economic History Review,* Vol. XV, Nos. 1 and 2: 1967.

Irschick, Eugene: *Dialogue and History: Constructing South India, 1795 - 1895.* Delhi: Oxford University Press, 1994.

"Occupational Diversification among Rural Groups" *Economic and Political Weekly,* 1997: 1908-1917.

Palanithurai, G, Ramesh R: *Globalisation and Rural Development.* New Delhi: Concept Publishing Company, 2010.

Papola, T S: "The Indian Labour Market." *Economic and Political Weekly*, 1968: 1179-82.

Reddy, Amarender: "Growth, Structural Change and Wage Rates in Rural India." *Economic and Political Weekly*, 2015: 56-65.

Samraj, Jerome C: "The Question of Land to the Dalits: A Historical Perspective." *Unpublished PhD thesis submitted to* Chennai, Tamil Nadu: University of 2009.

"Saving Agricultural Labour from Agriculture: SEZs and Politics of Silence in Tamil Nadu *Economic and Political Weekly"* 2010: 36-43.

Souza, Victor S D': "Social Inequalities and Development in India." *Economic and Political Weekly*, May 1975: 770-773.

"Special Economic Zones: Socio-economic Implications" *Economic and Political Weekly,* 2009: 18-21.

Notes

1. Heitzman, James (1987): 'Temple Urbanism in Medieval South India', Journal of Asian Studies 46 (4).
2. A report produced by the then Sub-Collector of Chingleput (present day Chengalpattu) titled 'Notes on Pariahs of Chingleput' would provide an in-depth understanding about the implications of land revenue policies of the colonial government in the Madras presidency. Also Irschick (1994) presents an interesting perspective on how the policy making and implementation during the colonial period was moderated by the local power structure that made it more of dialogic process rather than a dominant British colonial state imposing policies unilaterally.

3. See Ahuja: 1998 and also 'Depressed Classes and their Right to Land', Chapter 3, Part II in Jerome Samraj, C (2009), *The Question of Land to the Dalits: A Historical Perspective*, unpublished PhD thesis submitted to University of Madras, Chennai.
4. If a person has to shift to a formal salaried employment, he/she has to complete minimum ten years of formal education to reach the lowest cadre of formal employments which are categorised as Group D. Positions above these in the government and a lot other opportunities for formal employment in the private sectors needs a few more years of education.
5. Karshima, 1984.
6. For a more detailed account of the interaction between local society and the policy making during the colonial period read (Irschick 1994) and Samraj, C J (2009).
7. Basu (2004) and Samraj, C.J (2009).
8. http://www.thehindu.com/news/cities/chennai/firstyear-student-at-anna-university-commits-suicide/article3325338.ece
9. Cases of students from vulnerable social backgrounds committing suicide in higher education institutions due to 'academic' pressure and inability to cope up with the demands of studying in premier institutions may be worth recollecting Dhyriyalakshmi (Anna University 2012), Manivannan (Anna University, 2012), Senthil Kumar (University of Hyderabad, 2008), also see http://iitsuicides.blogspot.in/2011_06_01_archive.html. On most occasions, the institutions attributed such suicide to the student's poor performance in studies, however, never once the institutions have expressed scepticism over such reasoning as the same students have performed better in studies to gain admission in the same institution.
10. This can be sensed when we observe the government hostels, especially the welfare hostels for the Scheduled Castes, Scheduled Tribes, and also those for Backward Classes in cities where the hostels will always be over-crowded. Which indicates that the students who graduated cannot find suitable employment back in the native, and they are struggling to find a suitable employment in the cities. They can find one only by prolonging their stay in the cities for which they lack supportive social capital. This stands proof to the fact that the unequal system of education has put the deprived sections at a serious disadvantage because of their poor quality of schooling and disparity in their skills set compared to their fortunate others.
11. For a discussion on how the social inequalities determines people's access to development see D'Souza (1975). Saleth (1997) in his article on occupational diversification in Tamil Nadu presents a similar arguments by relating people and their access to land and their occupational diversification.

12. For a more detailed discussion on this read C. J. Fuller and Haripriya Narasimhan (2007), "Information Technology Professionals and the New-Rich Middle Class in Chennai (Madras)", *Modern Asian Studies*, Vol. 41, No. 1 (Jan., 2007), pp. 121-150. Also see C. J. Fuller and Haripriya Narasimhan (2006), "Engineering Colleges, 'Exposure' and Information Technology: Professionals in Tamil Nadu", *Economic and Political Weekly*, Vol. 41, No. 3 (Jan. 21-27, 2006), pp. 258-262+288.

12

A Revisit into B. R. Ambedkar's Perception on Caste

— *Kanak Kanti Bagchi*

"Among the numerous writings and speeches of Ambedkar that run into thousands of pages, The Annihilation of Caste is indeed his magnum opus. Judged by any criterion such as content, logic, argument, language, diction, exposition, urge and, above all, the force, it is a manifesto of social emancipation, and occupies a place similar to what The Communist Manifesto once did in the world communist movement"

— **Bhalchandra Mungekar**

Introduction

Pernicious effects of the caste system, prevalent in Hindu society, on the shudras and untouchables deeply shook the inner being of Babasaheb Bhimrao Ambedkar throughout his life from boyhood till his death. According to Ambedkar, "The caste problem is a vast one, both theoretically and practically. Practically, it is an institution that portends tremendous consequences.... Theoretically, it has defied a great many scholars who have taken upon themselves, as a labour of love, to dig into its origin" (Ambedkar, 1987). He himself suffered a lot for this unjust and inhuman system. He therefore vehemently fought for emancipating the dalits, the sufferers of this obnoxious system. By theoretical arguments and through empirical evidences he exposed the evils of the inhuman institution of caste.

There is no doubt that due to the caste system, dalits have remained socially degraded, economically impoverished and excluded from educational and cultural opportunities (Khalkho, n.d.). To restore their human dignity and give them a respectable place in society, Ambedkar struggled for about forty years and sought a religion that could liberate the depressed classes from the bondage of social evil. He wanted respect for dalits not as philanthropy but as a right and wanted to create the spirit of independence and self-reliance among them.

In his path breaking and in-depth analysis of on the problem of caste in his works 'Castes in India: Their Mechanisms, Genesis and Development', 'Annihilation of Caste', 'Who Are the Shudras', 'The Untouchables Who Were They and Why They Became Untouchables?' he has shown his profound scholarship. At the same time he had always been humble enough to be corrected if in his understanding of the subject if someone could convince him about the correctness of other view. In what follows we have analysed Ambedkar's perspective on caste based on his writings on the topic in the first two thesis written by him as noted above. The main objective of the present paper is to provide a critical appreciation of his views on caste and to comment on as to how much relevant are his diagnosis and prescription for solution of the problem in modern times.

This paper is structured as follows. Section I is introductory. Section II provides a brief review of literature. Methodology adopted for the study has been outlined in Section III. Section IV presents an analysis of Ambedkar's views on caste along with my comments on its relevance. Conclusions of the study have been drawn in Section V.

Review of Literature

Lots of studies have been done on Ambedkar's perspective on caste. We have selectively reviewed few of these works.

Jaffrelot (2009) has analysed the different aspects of the strategies of Ambedkar against untouchability and caste system. He has shown that Ambedkar has tried all kinds of strategies during his life for eradication of caste and, more especially, for emancipating the dalit from this oppressive social systems. Jaffrelot came to the conclusion that none of Ambedkar's strategies really succeeded during his life time: he could not have separate electorate introduced, he could not build a dalit or labour party, he could not have the Hindu code bill passed – and he became a bitter man.

Mungekar (n.d.) while reviewing Ambedkar's work 'Annihilation of Caste' has remarked that B. R. Ambedkar's passion for the abolition of untouchability and the eradication of caste is as relevant today as it was 75 years ago. He has made a brief but effective review of the points raised by Ambedkar in his work. Mungekar has also made an assessment on the relevance of Ambedkar's manifesto of social emancipation.

Kannibaran's (2009) study focuses on three texts by B. R. Ambedkar, M. N. Srinivas and Kancha Ilaiah that read together and in relation to each other speak to the sociology of caste in ways very different from hitherto canonical readings. She observes that these three texts when read in intersection, present rich possibilities both for an understanding of caste and more importantly for a re-examination of the sociology/legal ethnography of caste and its genealogy. The point that she found as interesting is the silence in the sociological work that emerged at that time and for at least five subsequent decades about Ambedkar's contribution to the sociology of caste.

According to Bemal (n.d.), Ambedkar, as a statesman, scholar, crusader of downtrodden and above all as a spiritual guide, has left an indelible impression on the Indian history. His contribution to uplift the downtrodden made him a cult figure among the depressed classes. He now lives in the heart and mind of the millions of the suffering people.

Patnaik (n.d.) opines that Ambedkar's critique of caste is premised on the centrality of caste as a structure of domination. He explains how domination is successful due to the reproductive roles of the state and religion. He also explains how Brahminism manages to penetrate to Dalit common sense so that caste domination manages to perpetuate. Caste is essentially about domination, for Ambedkar. Thereby, according to Patnaik, Ambedkar misses out to ask another series of central questions concerning caste. Moreover, Ambedkar's theory of caste based on the prime signifier of Brahminism is not adequate. Patnaik hold the view that non-Braminical ways of justifying caste are equally important for political and moral legitimating of caste.

Khalkho (n.d.) has dealt with Ambedkar's critique of the Indian social system. He has analysed the Hindu social system including the origin of caste and untouchability, Ambedkar's view and understanding of caste, shudras and untouchability, Ambedkar's idea of an ideal society and finally Ambedkar's rejection of Hinduism and embracing of Buddhism.

Hans (n.d.) has highlighted the present conditions and challenges of India's 167 million of oppressed and marginalised sections of society who have for thousands of years remained neglected and ignored in the social milieu. He maintains that despite political empowerment, dalits live in situations of social discrimination, physical violence and abject poverty. Around 50 per cent of the quantum of welfare measures is still unfulfilled. According to him, the focus now needs to be on dalit emancipation, rights and inclusive growth, both within 'dalitology' and the new pedagogy of inclusive growth.

Prabhakar (n.d.) in his study has made an attempt to understand the historical perspective of eradication of caste system in India and to elucidate B.R. Ambedkar's perspective about eradication of caste system in India. According to Prabhakar Ambedkar had done very eminent contribution of Jotiba Phule. Ambedkar's perspective on caste was developed not only by study but also through his experience.

Kumar's (n.d.) study deals with Ambedkar's critique of the caste system. It has six chapters. In third chapter he has dealt with Ambedkar's revolutionary ideas about the abolition of caste and social, economic and political reforms. The author has also laid some personal reflections on this issue. He feels that in the present day globalised world, the marginalised, downtrodden and dalits are victims of caste system. In this competitive world they suffer in two ways, first, they are not able to cope up with the situation and secondly, they are discriminated against. He feels that the only way to overcome the leprosy of caste system is to have mass education as well as to conscientiousness of the dalits.

Methodology

The study is based on both on primary and secondary sources of data and information. Ambedkar's own writings on caste, untouchability and shudra's are the primary source and articles written on these topics either on Ambedkar's idea about caste or written independently by authors are the secondary sources. We have mainly drawn on and analysed the views of Ambedkar on caste as revealed in his remarkable work 'Annihilation of Caste'.

Relook into Ambedkar's Outlook on Caste and its Relevance

Evils of the Caste System and the Need for Social Reform

The text of 'Annihilation of Caste' starts with the statement "Speech prepared by B. R. Ambedkar for the 1936 Annual Conference of the Jat-Pat-Todak Mandal of Lahore but not delivered owing to the cancellation of the Conference by the Reception Committee on the ground that the views expressed in the Speech would be unbearable to the Conference" (Ambedkar, 1936). But this address attracted the attention of Mahatma Gandhi and many caste Hindus and enlightened intellectuals, who were active in abolishing widowhood, child marriage etc but were not keen on abolishing the caste system as they did not have the courage to stand against it. Ambedkar invited the socialists to fight against the caste and he asserted that caste is not based on the division of labour. In his speech he urged upon the Hindus to annihilate the caste system, which according to him is a big hindrance to social solidarity, and to establish a new social order based on the ideals of liberty, equality and fraternity, and the principles of democracy. He suggested that the institutions of society must be based on reason and not on atrocious traditions (*Ibid*). In this way, the speech consistently suggested various methodical steps to annihilate the whole caste system and to reform Hinduism.

According to Ambedkar, in a caste-ridden society like India political reform should be preceded by social reform. But "the path of social reform like the path to heaven at any rate in India, is strewn with many difficulties. Social reform in India has few friends and many critics" (*Ibid*). He was closely observing how around 1890s and later there was a gradual decline of the strength of importance of the Social Conference wing of the National Congress. He held the view that social reform had a great bearing on political reform. He then citing evidences of the inhuman treatment of the untouchables by the high caste Hindus in India asked the following questions: "Are you fit for political power even though you do not allow a large class of your countrymen like the untouchables to use public school? Are you fit for political power even though you do not allow them to use of public wells? Are you fit for political power even though you do not allow them to use of public streets? Are you fit for political power even though you do not allow them to wear what apparel or ornaments they like? Are you fit for political power even though you do not allow them to eat any food they like?" (*Ibid*). In the then contemporary reality there was really no affirmative answer to these questions from a sensible man.

He made a distinction between social reform in the sense of the reorganisation and reconstruction of the Hindu Society. "The former has relation to widow remarriage, child marriage etc., while the latter relates to the abolition of the caste system. The Social Conference was a body which mainly concerned itself with the reform of the high caste Hindu family. It consisted mostly of enlightened high caste Hindus who did not feel the necessity for agitating for the abolition of caste or had not the courage to agitate for it". Thus, according to Ambedkar the battle that was fought by the Social Conference was centred round the question of the reform of the family. It did not relate to the social reform in the sense of the break-up of the caste system. Ambedkar alluded to the social and religious movements that did precede over political revolution in other countries of the world and in India over the ages. He then came to the conclusion that 'the emancipation of the mind and the soul is a necessary/preliminary for the political expansion of the people' (*Ibid*).

Situation in contemporary India has changed a lot. Now untouchables can use public schools. There is no restriction in the use of public wells by dalits. There is no unfreedom in using public streets by untouchables. There is no restriction imposed by upper castes to use apparel or ornaments by scheduled castes. Dalits can now take food they like subject to availability without any restriction imposed by upper castes. But it has taken about six decades after the death of Ambedkar to reach at this stage, though the achievement is not yet fully satisfactory.

As far as social reform is concerned reorganisation of Hindu society has taken place. Window re-marriage is a common thing nowadays. However, even though the incidence of child marriage in no longer there among upper castes, it may be prevalent to some extent among dalits. But the matter of concern is that incidence of marriage below the legally permitted age of girls is still happening among the poor dalits which needs a remedy.

As far as the issue of reconstruction of Hindu Society is concerned, currently no political party has the agenda of abolishing caste system among Hindus. Political parties remain indifferent to the question of reform in any religion. Even with the so-called socialist or communist parties there is no agenda for eradicating the caste system. Rather sometimes they also use caste as a strategy for winning election.

Criticising the Socialists Position

He has also criticised the Socialists for their overemphasis on viewing humans as economic beings. Socialists advocate that man is an economic creature, that his activities and aspirations are bound by economic facts, that property is the only source of power. They, therefore, preach that economic reform by equalisation of property must have precedence over political and social reform. According to Ambedkar, "that economic reform is the only kind of power no student of human society can accept. That the social status of an individual by itself often becomes a source of power and authority is made clear by the sway which the Mahatmas have held over the common man" (*Ibid*). He alluded to examples from India and European countries to show how in some instances religion was a source of power than money?

Ambedkar held that at that time the Socialists in India did not have considered the question of the impossibility of bringing economic reform without first bringing about a reform of the social order. He argued that economic reform contemplated by the Socialists cannot come about unless there is a revolution resulting in seizure of power. That seizure of power must be by a proletariat. Here, Ambedkar raises the question whether the proletariats of India combine to bring about this revolution. Men will not join in a revolution for the equalisation of property unless they know that after revolution is achieved they will be treated equally and that there will be no discrimination of caste and creed. Ambedkar felt that the assurance of a socialist leading the revolution that he does not believe in caste must be the assurance proceeding from much deeper foundation, namely, the mental attitude of the compatriots towards one another in their spirit of personal equality and fraternity. He then puts four crucial questions: 'Can it be said that the poor in India recognise no such distinctions of caste or creed, high or low? If the fact that they do, what unity of front can be expected from such a proletariat in its action against the rich? How can there be a revolution if the proletariat cannot present a united front?' Ambedkar's firm belief was that even if by some freak of fortune a revolution does take place and the Socialists come to power, they will be compelled to take account of caste after revolution if he does not take account of it before revolution. Thus, according to him in order to have economic reform or political reform the monster of caste is to be killed.

In the post-independence period communists could come to power only in three states, namely, West Bengal, Tripura and Kerala. In these three states for certain reasons caste discrimination or caste feeling is probably less compared to other states of India. But in these states also dalits are not entirely free from discrimination. If these states could set an example that due to communist rule economic as well as social inequalities have been removed then dalits of other states could support the communist parties in election in those states. But unfortunately, no such example has been set by the communist parties. That may be one of the reasons as to why except these three states communists could not make any inroads among voters of other states. Thus, it proves the correctness of Ambedkar's prophecy that dalits are to be taken into confidence about their chances of attaining social equality after the communist parties get elected.

Caste as Division of Labour – Refutation of the Argument

Defenders defend caste system on the ground that it indicates division of labour. Since division of labour is a necessary feature of every civilised society, therefore, there is nothing wrong in the caste system. This view has been severely criticised by Ambedkar on the following grounds. First, for the reason that caste system is not merely division of labour, it is also a division of labourers. In Indian society division of labour is accompanied by this unnatural division of labourers into watertight compartments.

Secondly, to Ambedkar, caste system is not merely a division of labourers which is quite different from division of labour. It is actually a hierarchy in which the division of labourers are graded one above the other. He felt that in no other country is the division of labour accompanied by this gradation of labourers.

Thirdly, this division of labour is not spontaneous. It is not based on natural aptitudes. The caste system involves an attempt to appoint tasks to individuals in advance, selected not on the basis of trained original capacities, but on that of the social status of the parents.

Fourthly, stratification of occupations on the basis of caste system is positively pernicious. Industry is never static and it undergoes rapid and sudden changes and therefore an individual must be free to change his occupation. But the caste system would not allow Hindus to take to occupations where they are wanted if they do not belong to them by heredity.

According to Ambedkar, by not permitting readjustment of occupations, caste becomes a direct cause of much of the unemployment we see in the country.

Ambedkar further added that as a form of division of labour the caste system suffers from another serious defect. The division of labour brought about by the caste system is not a division based on choice. Individual sentiment, individual preference has no place in it. It is based on the dogma of predestination.

Elaborating this point further he noted that considerations of social efficiency would compel us to recognise that the greatest evil in the industrial system is not so much poverty and the suffering that it involves as the fact that so many persons have callings which make no appeal to those who are engaged in them. Consequently, such callings constantly provoke one to aversion, ill will and the desire to evade.

So he raised the pertinent question: "What efficiency can there be in a system under which neither men's hearts nor their minds are in their work?" (*Ibid*). He therefore came to the conclusion that as an economic organisation Caste is a harmful institution, inasmuch as it involves the subordination of man's natural powers and inclinations to the exigencies of social rules.

Division of labour is a basic characteristic of an industrial organisation. That caste system indicates division of labour is neither morally acceptable and nor desirable at any time as argued by Ambedkar. In present time affirmative action in the form of reservation of job in the government sector has been introduced for SC/ST/OBC candidates. The practice of following traditional occupation by dalits has declined to a great extent. Now they have the freedom to choose callings according to the level of education, skill and training attained by them. There is no evidence that reservation of job for dalits resulted in lower efficiency or productivity in economic activities. It proves that caste system is pernicious to economic growth and social development.

Biological Reason of Caste – Refutation of the Argument

Ambedkar has also refuted the biological reasons for defending the caste system. Preservation of purity of race and purity of blood is put as a reason for maintaining the caste system. Ethnologists are of opinion that men of pure race exist nowhere and that there has been a mixture of all races in all parts of the world. In this context he has quoted Bhandarkar who stated that "there is hardly a class, or caste in India which has not a foreign strain in it. There is an admixture of alien blood not only among the warrior classes - the Rajputs and the Marathas – but also among the Brahmins who are under the happy delusion that they are free from all foreign elements" (Bhandarkar, D. R.: *Foreign Elements in the Hindu Population*, quoted in Ambedkar) (*Ibid*).

Ambedkar was therefore of the opinion that the caste system cannot be said to have grown as a means of preventing the admixture of races or as a means of maintaining purity of blood. As a matter of fact, caste system came into being long after the different races of India had commingled in blood and culture. To hold that distinctions of castes or really distinctions of race and to treat different castes as though there were so many different races is a gross perversion of facts. Caste system is a social division of people of the same race.

The effect of caste on the ethics of the Hindus, according to Ambedkar is simply deplorable. He opined that caste has killed public spirit, the sense of public charity and made public opinion impossible. A Hindu's public is his caste. His responsibility is only to his caste. His loyalty is restricted only to his caste. Virtue has become casteridden and morality has become caste-bound. There is no sympathy to the deserving. There is no appreciation of the meritorious. There is no charity to the needy. Suffering as such calls for no response. There is charity but it begins with the caste and ends with the caste. There is sympathy but not for men of other caste. There is appreciation of virtue but only when the man is a fellow caste-man. On the point of ethics, therefore he put a crucial question: "Have not Hindus committed treason against their country in the interests of their caste?" (*Ibid*).

Ambedkar's critique of the caste system on the ground of biological reasons and his depiction of the pernicious effect of caste on the ethics of the Hindus is quite valid till now.

Caste System and Elements of Ambedkar's Ideal Society

Ambedkar said that his ideal society would be based on *Liberty, Equality and Fraternity*. An ideal society according to him should be mobile, should be full of channels for conveying change taking place in one part to other parts. In an ideal society there should be many interests consciously communicated and shared. There should be varied and free points of contact with other modes of association. This is fraternity, which is another name for democracy. It is essentially an attitude of respect and reverence towards fellow men.

According to him some people object to liberty in the sense of a right to free movement, in the sense of a right to life and limb. But there is no objection to liberty in the sense of a right to property, tools and materials as being necessary for earning a living to keep the body in due state of health. He opined that liberty should be allowed to benefit by an effective and competent use of a person's powers. But he felt that the supporters of caste who would not allow liberty in the sense of a right to life, limb and property, would not readily consent to liberty in this sense, inasmuch as it involves liberty to choose one's profession. He believed that to object to this kind of liberty is to perpetuate slavery. He considered that slavery does not merely mean a legalised form of subjection. It means a state of society in which some men are forced to accept from the other the purposes which control their conduct. This condition obtains even where there is no slavery in the legal sense. It is found where, as in the caste system, some persons are compelled to carry on certain prescribed occupations which are not of their choice.

Regarding equality his opinion was that 'equality may be a fiction but nonetheless one must accept it as the governing principle'. According to him, a man's power is dependent upon physical heredity, social inheritance or endowment which enables him to be more efficient than the savage, and thirdly, on his own efforts. In all these respects men are undoubtedly unequal. But he puts the question: "Shall we treat them as unequal because they are unequal?" (*Ibid*). He considered that from the standpoint of the individualist it may be just to treat men unequally so far as their efforts are unequal. To address the situation his prescription was that, "it may be desirable to give as much as possible to the full development of every one's powers" (*Ibid*). He asserted that for the same reason in the first two respects we should treat men as equally as possible. At the same time he recommended that if it is good for the social body to get most out of its members, it can get most out of them only by making them equal as far as possible at the very start of the race. That is one reason why equality cannot be escaped.

The other reason according to him is that "however desirable or reasonable an equitable treatment of men may be, humanity is not capable of assortment and classification. The statesman, therefore, must follow some rough and ready rule and that rough and ready rule is to treat all men alike not because they are alike but because classification and assortment is impossible" (*Ibid*). According to him the doctrine of equality is glaringly fallacious but taking all in all it is the only way a statesman can proceed in politics which is a severely practical affair and which demands a severely practical test.

I think the idea of an ideal society based on liberty, equality and fraternity as outlined by Ambedkar is still valid and would remain so for ever.

Abolition of Caste

Ambedkar was convinced that unless social order is changed little can be achieved by way of progress. Nothing can be built on the foundations of caste. His considered opinion was that building up a nation and building up a morality cannot be done on the foundations of caste. Anything built on the foundations of caste will crack and will never be a whole.

He was concerned with the question, how to abolish caste? This was a question of supreme importance to him. He has given concrete suggestions for the abolition of caste and the establishment of society based on true liberty, equality and fraternity.

He critically explored the various ways in which caste can be abolished. He first dealt with the view that in the reform of caste, the first step to take is to abolish sub-castes. But he was not in favour of this view. He argued that even if by assumption fusion of sub-castes is possible, what guarantee is there that the abolition of sub-castes will necessarily lead to the abolition of castes? On the contrary, it may happen that the process may stop with the abolition of sub-castes. In that case, the abolition of sub-castes will only help to strengthen the castes and make them more powerful and therefore more harmful. According to him, this remedy is neither practicable nor effective and may easily prove to be a wrong remedy.

The second plan of action for the abolition of caste is to begin with inter-caste dinners. He felt that it is also an inadequate remedy. He was of the opinion that there are many castes which allow interdining. But the common experience is that inter-dining has not succeeded in killing the spirit of caste and the consciousness of caste. He was convinced that the real remedy for the abolition of caste is inter-marriage. Fusion of blood can alone create the feeling of being kith and kin and unless this feeling of kinship becomes paramount, the feeling of being aliens created by caste will not vanish. He felt that the real remedy for breaking caste is inter-marriage. Nothing else will serve as the solvent of caste.

While congratulating the Jat-Pat-Todak Mandal for correct diagnosis of the disease Ambedkar asked the Mandal as to 'Why is it that a large majority of Hindus do not inter-dine and do not inter-marry?' In answering the question he said that inter-dining and inter-marriage are repugnant to the beliefs and dogmas which the Hindus regard as sacred. They observe caste because they are deeply religious. People are not wrong in observing caste. In his view, what is wrong is their religion, which has inculcated this notion of caste. Ambedkar observed that if this view is correct, then obviously the enemy is not the people who observe caste, but the Shastras which teach them this religion of caste. The real remedy, according to him is to destroy the belief in the sanctity of the Shastras.

According to Ambedkar, reason and morality are two most important weapons in the weapon store of a reformer. To deprive him of the use of these weapons is akin to disabling him for action. He raised the question, 'How are you going to break up caste, if people are not free to consider whether it accords with reason? How are you going to break up caste if people are not free to consider whether it accords with morality?' He further diagnosed the problem and noted that the wall build around caste is impregnable and the material, of which it is built, contains none of the combustible stuff of reason and morality. He adds that inside this wall stands the army of Brahmins, who form the intellectual class, Brahmins who are the natural leaders of the Hindus and the former are there not as mercenary soldiers but as an army fighting for its homeland and that is why breaking-up of caste amongst the Hindus is almost impossible.

According to him the priestly caste "is a pest which divinity seems have let loose on the masses for their mental and moral degradation" (*Ibid*). He had vehemently criticised the profession of Hindu priesthood, pointed out its defects and suggested its reform to prevent it from doing mischief and from misguiding people. He held that 'it will certainly kill the Braminism and will also help to kill caste, which is nothing but Brahminism incarnate'. Brahminism is the poison which has spoiled Hinduism and Hinduism would be saved if Brahminism is killed.

Under such the situation as described by him, he was a little pessimistic and observed that it would take ages before a breach is made. However, whether the achievement of abolition of caste takes time or done quickly, he suggested not to forget that in order to bring about a breach in the caste system the dynamite is to be applied "to the Vedas and the Shastras, which deny any part to reason, and to Vedas and Shastras, which deny any part to morality" (*Ibid.* The religion of the Shrutis and the Smritis must be destroyed. This was his considered view of the matter.

During Ambedkar's time this remedy was partially relevant. There is the need for rejecting those parts of Shastras and Vedas which talked about casteism, instead of rejecting these altogether. And also there is the need for reform in the structure of Hinduism. Now, probably with the passage of time majority of Hindus have started rejecting those parts of Vedas and Shastras which discriminates among human beings. I think inter-caste marriage is still a very much valid way of abolishing caste. It is happening in India very slowly. It is to be promoted, popularised and encouraged at individual, social and national level by all castes and communities and at government level also by providing incentives for such marriages.

Conclusion

In conclusion it can be said that Ambedkar's fight against the injustices perpetrated by the caste system on the dalits and his struggle for the abolition of caste system has not gone in vain. There has been some definite gain. Some dent has been made in the process of abolition of caste. But there are miles to go. Spread of quality education among the dalits and destitute can be the most potent way of eradicating the caste system. Of course, the mind set of upper castes as well as dalits need to be changed and the sense of meaningless of caste system is to prevail among all. How that can be brought about is a million dollar question and it is the proper answer to this question by the society which is the need of the hour on which progress, peace and prosperity of the nation depends.

References

Ambedkar, B. R. (1916, reprint 2009). *Castes in India: Their Mechanism, Genesis and Development*. Delhi: Siddhartha Books.

Ambedkar, B. R. (1987). *Annihilation of Caste*. Bangalore: Dalit Sahitya Academy.

Bemal, Tofan (2008). B. R. Ambedkar, Crusader Against Caste and Untouchability of Hindu Social Order. Orissa Review, pp. 19-28.

Hans, Basil V. (n.d.). Dalits in India: From Marginalisation to Inclusion. Retrieved from www.themenplattform-ez.de/wp-content/uploads/2013/02/SSRN-id2323268.pdf

Jaffrelot, Christophe (2009). Ambedkar's Strategies Against Untouchability and the Caste System. Indian Institute of Dalit Studies. Working Paper Series, Vol. III, Number 04, pp.1-23.

Kannibaran, Kalpana (2009). Sociology of Caste and the Crooked Mirror: Recovering B R Ambedkar's Legacy. *Economic and Political Weekly,* January 24, pp. 35-39.

Khalkho, Prabhu Narayan (n.d.). Ambedkar's Critique of the Indian Social System. Retrieved from http://snphilosophers2005.tripod.com/prabhu.pdf

Kumar, Dilip (n.d.). Ambedkar's Critique of the Caste System. Retrieved from http://snphilosophers2005.tripod.com/dilip.pdf

Mungekar, Bhalchandra (n.d.). Annihilation of Caste – A Review. Retrieved from http://www.frontline.in/static/html/fl2815/stories/20110729281509500.htm

Patnaik, Arun K (n.d.). Ambedkar's Annihilation of Caste: A Textual Reading. Retrieved from https://castecritics.files.wordpress.com/2012/03/75th-anniversary-of-annihilating-caste1.pdf

Prabhakar, R., Nisargandh (n.d.). Eradication of Caste System in India: A Perspective of Dr B. R. Ambedkar. Retrived from

https://www.academia.edu/8454793/Eradication_of_Caste_System_in_India_ A_perspective_of_Dr. B.R. Ambedkar

Venmalottu (Roji), Bro. Kurien (n.d.). Befriending the Other: A Study About Hindu Caste System. Retrived from

https://www.academia.edu/19604586/Befriending_the_other_A_study_on_Hindu_caste_system

Index